Philippe Bauduin · Jean-Charles Stasi

D-DAY

What we haven't told you...

Texts: Philippe Bauduin and Jean-Charles Stasi

Coordination: Jean-Charles Stasi

Translation: Lawrence Brown

Layout: Paul Gros

Colour profiles: Thierry Vallet, Jacques Clémentine

Photographic sources: Philippe Bauduin collection, Jean-Charles Stasi collection, Heimdal archives , British archives (IWM, National Archives), American archives (NARA), German archives (Bundesarchiv), CCVOL-Breton Resistance Museum, war archives-Dominique Forget, Grand Bunker Museum (Ouistreham), Musée Grand Bunker-Fonds Lesage, N°4 Commando Museum (Ouistreham), Vincent Dussutour collection, Jean-Bernard Frappé, Francis Cormon, Jacques Clémentine, Thierry Vallet, Patrick Collet collection, François Robinard collection, Stéphane Jacquet collection, Corinne and Gérard Liard collection, Michaël Fuller collection, Smithonian ASM archives, Schloesing family archives, Erich Sommer collection.

Éditions Heimdal

BP 61350 - 14406 BAYEUX Cedex

Tél: 02.31.51.68.68   Fax: 02.31.51.68.60

E-mail: editions.heimdal@wanadoo.fr

www.editions-heimdal.fr

PUBLISHER'S INTRODUCTION
What we haven't told you...

Publishers and authors since 1975, our first books concerning the Battle of Normandy were first published in 1976. In the decades that have followed, knowledge concerning this battle has considerably evolved. Interest had been fuelled by the book, then the film, *The Longest Day*, but also by Paul Carel's Sie Kommen that gave the German viewpoint. However, general knowledge was limited to clichés, or sometimes false truths. The most mysterious fact remained that of the number of civilian casualties, something that we can now put a precise number to and which will at last be spoken of in a new museum opening in Falaise in 2016. There were more than 20,000 civilian deaths in Normandy, a higher number than British soldiers; it is a terrible figure. Since, the false truths have partially collapsed. The film, *The Longest Day*, began with one. We see Major Pluskat, in his coastal command bunker, as he first sees the allied fleet. We now know that he lied; he was not there at dawn on 6 June, but was with a lady friend in Caen... There are many examples of such stories. With the veterans fading away into history, the knowledge concerning this battle is being considerably reviewed and enriched. This book takes a look at a lesser known aspect, what still remains secret or barely spoken of.

Among the great 'secrets' of the landings one must bring up a paradoxical subject, that of the role played by the German high command in the allied victory.

Did the Germans know?

Before anything else, we should remember that the German command was torn between different trains of thought – Rommel did not agree with von Rundstedt and von Schweppenburg concerning the placement of armoured divisions. Rommel wanted them to be close to the coast in order to carry an immediate counter-attack against the beaches, but he was only partially listened to. But which beaches? Most of the German generals expected the Allies to land in the Pas-de-Calais and the success of Operation Fortitude's contribution to the allied success is mentioned. The Germans had been hoodwinked over the final objective, believing it to be the Pas-de-Calais, not imagining the possibility of landings in Normandy. However, the truth is not so straightforward... as Hubert Meyer showed as early as 1991, Hitler and Rommel believed in the possibility of landings in Normandy; that is why several divisions were sent there as reinforcements. This was first the case with the *91. (Luftlande) Infanterie-Division* which only arrived mid-May 1944, something that forced the American

A German propaganda photograph showing a German coastal artillery soldier in front of an Atlantic Wall casemate. This was only partially the reality.

Another propaganda photo taken near Dieppe. A soldier disappears into an underground tunnel of a veritable fortress. However, the "Wall" was a fortress in name only.

2.Panzer-Division (2). When field marshal Rommel became inspector of the Atlantic Wall in November 1943, he was shocked by the lack of beach defences. Apart from the heavy Pas-de-Calais defences that had been filmed and photographed by German propaganda services, or a few coastal artillery batteries, the "Wall" in Normandy was nothing but an illusion (3). Often, a few logs were all that fortified a small beach defensive position. Rommel thus intensified work and the "Wall" only began to really take shape between the end of 1943 and... 6 June 1944. When the allied troops landed, many casemates were still not completed or dry. In a troop bunker at WN62 in the future Omaha Beach sector, water running down the walls and the soldiers that slept there were tormented by the smell of cement. Thanks to Rommel, the "Wall" began to pose a real threat, even if it was far from being finished. The losses suffered by the Americans at Omaha Beach and the Canadians at Courseulles and Graye back this fact up. However, at Omaha Beach, the topography and a totally failed preparatory bombardment helped the German defenders. As for the Canadians, the still light defences show the extent to which they could have been formidable. Also, the efficiency of the allied bombing had forced the Germans to remove their artillery pieces from their emplacements which allowed them to fire in all directions, and put them in casemates, thus considerably reducing their field of fire. Thus, the batteries at Longues and at the Pointe du Hoc, for example, no longer threatened the beaches but rather the fleet out at sea. Added to this, at the Pointe du Hoc, the artillery pieces were hidden in a sunken lane to the rear of the position as the work on the casemates was not completed; the attack on the position was heroic but doubly pointless... As for the troops manning the "Wall" and the coastal strip, these were static units of poor military quality, 30% of which was made up of "Eastern" volunteers, former Soviet citizens and prisoners of

command, on 26 May 1944, to totally modify its plan for the airborne operation in the Cotentin, just a few days before Overlord (1) ; its two airborne would be grouped together at Sainte-Mère-Église and Sainte-Marie du-Mont, with the crossing of the crossing of the La Fière causeway and subsequently a tougher fight. There was an even bigger surprise at Omaha Beach with the discovery of General Kraiss's *352.Infanterie-Division* opposing the landing of the American troops. Present in the Normandy bocage since June 1942, this unit had been moved closer to the beach a short time before the landings and its unforeseen presence in the sector had almost led to an American disaster at Omaha Beach.

However, despite Rommel's requests, the panzer divisions would remain far from the Normandy coastline, with the exception of the

(1) See Georges Bernage, *Objectif Carentan*, Heimdal, 2010, p.5.

(2) See G. Bernage, *Les Panzers face au débarquement*, Heimdal, 2012.

(3) See G. Bernage, *Le Mur de l'Atlantique en Normandie*, Heimdal, 2011.

war, but also real volunteers who had enlisted with the Germans to fight Stalin, but who had also been placed there for a fight that was not theirs. This did not stop the Georgians of the 795th Battalion putting up an energetic fight until 7 June before capitulating and finally being handed over to Stalin, like all of the "Ost" soldiers, victims of cold allied cynicism. The fact remains that the landing troops were surprised to encounter Georgians, Russians, Turkmen and other Soviet citizens fighting alongside the Germans and this is another lesser known aspect of the D-Day story. In fact, "did the Germans know?". It would appear that yes, they did. Let us quote two stories. At around 8 p.m. on Monday 5 June 1944, Bernardin Birette, a 20 year-old farmer's son from Audouville-la-Hubert, a village close to Sainte Mère-Eglise, and the sea, arrived at the family farm, occupied by Georgians of the 795th Battalion, and found himself near the crossroads of the Virgin Mary. It was there, accompanied by Edouard Pergeaux, that they saw two German flak soldiers arrive by bicycle and stop near an electrical transformer opposite the Virgin Mary. One of the soldiers climbed onto the transformer, cut off the electricity then removed two fuses that he attached to a thin rope and passed down to his companion. He then climbed back down and got back on his bike. This was a strange thing to be doing and Bernardin Birette asked the German what he was doing, receiving the reply as the soldier rode off *"Monzieur fini elektrik!"*. *"But why?"* asked the young Normandy farmhand. As the German disappeared off down the road he shouted back in French *"Perhaps there will be big trouble tonight!"* (4) As for the "famous" Major Pluskat, he had made the strange remark to several of his officers on 2 June 1944 that, when the long-awaited attack came, they were to pull back as quickly as possible. (5) Stranger still is the account by Rudolf von Ribbentrop, the son of the Reich foreign minister, a Panther tank troop commander at the time with the *12.SS-Panzer-Division "Hitlerjugend"*. At the end of the morning of 3 June 1944, he had been wounded in the lung by fire from an allied fighter-bomber as he was moving along a road in the Eure department following a night exercise. He was taken to the Bernay hospital. It was there, that on Sunday 4 June, he received a visit from the German ambassador in Paris, sent by his father to enquire on his son's condition: *"He told me that the latest intelligence was predicting the allied landings for 5 June. When he said goodbye to me on the morning of 5 June as he was leaving for Paris in his Holzkocher car, I laughingly said to him that still nothing had happened, to which he*

---

(4) See G. Bernage, *Utah Beach*, Heimdal, pp.58 et 69.

(5) Hein Severloh, *WN62*, Heimdal, p.50.

Watching from an artillery observation post, whilst some of the German high command "knew" and that the alert was given too late.

dryly and quite rightly replied, "the day is not over yet!". *It was during the night of 5-6 June that they arrived! Rommel, the commander of the army of which we were part, was with his family in Germany".* **(6)** Thus, the Germans did know, but... Part of the high command wanted to see the defeat of the 3rd Reich, and of Germany, and knowingly helped the Allies carry out their plan. We have all heard of Operation Valkyrie, the assassination attempt on Hitler on 20 July 1944. But, without going into the details, let us remind ourselves of the role played by Admiral Canaris, the head of the German *Abwehr* counter-espionage services who had wilfully misled the high command,

but also that of General Speidel, Rommel's chief of staff who explained, after the war, his role in holding back vital information. In his book on the *12.SS-Panzer-Division* **(7)**, Hubert Meyer shows with accuracy how, as Chester Wilmot stated, false intelligence transmitted by the Fremde Heere West services, led to decisive errors. Despite the incredible courage of the German soldier who resisted for almost three months in the Normandy bocage, the allied high command had an ultra-top secret weapon: part of the German high command. To end with a final anecdote, in 1977, General von Schwerin, who had commanded the *116. Panzer-Division*, told me **(8)** something that had never been said before in that his division had been told to stay put north of the Seine until the end of the July 1944, instead of being sent into battle as early as 7 June, in order to remain at the disposal of the 20 July plotters...

Georges Bernage
publisher and historian

(6) See G. Bernage's article, *"La compagnie von Ribbentrop à Harcourt"*, *Normandie 1944*, n°15, p.8.

(7) Chester Wilmot, *The Struggle for Europe and Hubert Meyer, 12.SS-Panzer-Division*, Heimdal, 1991, pp.25, 92 and 93.

(8) See G. Bernage, *Le couloir de la mort*, Heimdal, 2016 (3rd edition), p.42.

Even at the future Omaha Beach sector, several casemates were still undergoing construction at WN66 on the evening of 5 June...

INTRODUCTION
D-Day seen in a new light

More than seventy years after the events, the Normandy Landings continue to fascinate, as much by the feats of imagination employed, the audacity and courage shown by its planners and those who took part, as well as its historical importance and symbolic dimension (the beginning of the end of the Second World War). Despite the fact that it has been the subject of a great many studies, there still remain aspects that are unknown or little known to the public. The aim of this book is to shine a light on some of these stories, but also to provide an answer to questions that are still pending. Thus, were there radars near Pegasus Bridge in order to guide the glider tow planes? Why did the attack at Pointe du Hoc go ahead when the 155 mm guns had been moved a few days previously? Why is it that the incredible mathematician Alan Turing is never mentioned in the memoirs of the main allied leaders? These are just some of the many questions that can only serve to increase the interest of the wider public, as well as those with a passion for this enormous event. Will we one day learn of the new and emerging technology that was tested out in Normandy during this period: mobile telephones, jet planes, infra-red goggles, streptomycin or the blood plasma-filled shells fired by artillery etc.? Is it possible to believe that the young combatants on both sides fought each other whilst listening to the same song: *Lili Marleen* for the Germans, *Lilli Marlene* for the Allies? We hope that these revelations, explanations and questions will help readers of all ages to cast a new light on D-Day and the Battle of Normandy.

Philippe Bauduin and Jean-Charles Stasi

1. Lily Sergueiew, The Germans' trump card... and that of the Allies

Known as "Solange" to the *Abwehr* and "Treasure" for the British intelligence services, the beautiful and enigmatic spy, Lily Sergueiew, was considered by both sides as being their best agent in London in the months prior to the Landings.

There is, without doubt, something of an Indiana Jones in a skirt concerning this woman of boundless energy and incredible cheek, born in Petrograd (today known as Saint Petersburg) on 25 January 1912. She was still a child when her parents arrived in Paris a short time after the Russian Revolution of 1917. A few years later she became a pupil at the Académie Julian, a private art and sculpture school. However, apart from this attraction for art, Lily was filled with a great desire to see the world.

In July 1933, she set off on foot for Warsaw. The insatiable curiosity of this young French woman, travelling alone and easily recognizable by her pale complexion, backpack and large hobnailed walking boots, soon caught the attention of the new regime in power in Germany. Had she not requested a meeting with von Papen, a member of the Führer's cabinet? Had she not managed to get herself sent to a labour camp for two days for having camped outside the propaganda ministry?

Before continuing her route eastwards, she met someone who would play an important role in her life: Félix Dassel. This journalist with a Berlin daily newspaper showed an interest in her sketches and asked her questions – a lot of questions, she ended up thinking – concerning what she thought about the new Germany and its leaders.

When war broke out, the adventurer found herself in Aleppo, Syria, as she was on her way, by bicycle, to Saigon. After waiting for several months, she returned to France in November 1940 on board a liner crammed with demobbed soldiers.

Below: Felix Dassel, the German journalist that Lily met in Berlin in 1933. They would meet again a few years later in Paris...

Lily Sergueiew's identity card, born in Russia and made a French citizen.

A few months before war broke out, Lily Sergueiew left Paris under a guard of honour for her bicycle trip that was to take her to Saigon.

A short time after her return to Paris she was on the verge of falling prey to poverty and the rigors of the first winter under occupation. Therefore, she got back in touch with Félix Dassel who, as well as being a press correspondent, was also a recruiter for the *Abwehr*, the military intelligence agency of the German supreme command, led by Admiral Canaris. *"I'm fed up! Fed up! I've had enough of starving, enough of freezing!"* She blurted out to Dassel as a justification for her choice, which was somewhat surprising given that it meant working for the enemy.

Lily worked hard, beginning her apprenticeship between intensive courses in Paris and stays in Berlin. She was shown how to write messages in invisible ink and sending messages in Morse code, all the time whilst staying in apartments and hotel rooms.

When her training was completed, she was given the code name of *"Solange"* and placed under the command of an Austrian officer, Major Emile Kliemann. The latter soon saw the potential in his new recruit and had only one idea: to send her as quickly as possible to England. This was, however, easier said than done without catching the attention of the numerous British intelligence agents in France, as well as the rest of Europe. After a very long wait of two years, punctuated with periods of low morale, Lily at last climbed on to a train for Spain at the end of June 1943, accompanied by her small dog, Babs. The objective in Spain was to acquire a visa for England via Gibraltar.

Two weeks after arriving in Madrid, Lily was called to the British consulate concerning her request.

— So if I have understood correctly, you would like to go to England in order to be reunited with your family... the civil servant in charge of passports began.

The answer given by the young French woman left him speechless:

— Not exactly. I'm going there to spy.

A sketch by Lily Sergueiew, showing her during questioning by the German secret police in October 1933 when she was imprisoned in Berlin.

Spring 1944, Lisbon. Lily Sergueiew and Major Kliemann, her *Abwehr* handler.

Placed under the orders of Lieutenant-Colonel Robertson, with Mary Sheerer as her direct handler she was given the code name of *"Treasure"*. Throughout the following months, her work consisted of sending false intelligence to Major Kliemann whilst all the time being careful not to arouse his suspicion.

Up to the spring of 1944, Lily transmitted from London to the *Abwehr*, Morse code messages designed to fool the Germans as to the landing preparations. This was all part of Operation Fortitude, a huge plan concerning false intelligence.

During this period, she frequently travelled to Portugal to speak directly to Kliemann who, not suspecting anything, showed an increasing satisfaction in her work, seeing her as one of his best agents. At each meeting, the Major presented her with new requests concerning the landings which appeared imminent, but whose precise date and place remained desperately unknown to the Germans. *"If you can say that the Bristol – Salisbury Sector is quiet or, on the contrary, full of troops and buzzing with activity, we will know where the enemy is preparing to land. Lily, I don't believe that a woman has ever had such an opportunity to change the course of history..."* Kliemann said to her on 22 March 1944, with a seriousness that was more marked than usual.

The weeks leading up to the Landings proved to be more and more difficult for Lily. The serious kidney stones that she had been diagnosed with in January weakened her more and more with each passing day and at the same time affected her morale. Her relationship with Lieutenant-Colonel Robertson and Mary Sherer, who she called Mariya, rapidly deteriorated and Lily increasingly suffered from loneliness, reproaching her handling officers with being too cold towards her.

The young woman, whom doctors said only had a few months to live, threatened the British with sabotaging her work by transmitting without indicating her security check word *"pianist"* which allowed the Germans to see that she was not being forced to send Morse code messages.

No longer fully trusting her, the British Intelligence Service ended up side-lining her shortly before D-Day. This is despite the fact that

In one go, Lily told everything to the civil servant, Benton, a man she knew nothing about, starting with her first contact with Dassel in Berlin ten years previously, and up to her spy mission concerning the preparations of allied landings in Europe, not omitting her long training period in Paris.

What she had to say was even more interesting to the British given that Major Kliemann, as Benton said, *"is one of the German espionage's big bosses"*. Thus, before she had even set foot in England, Lily had gone from being a spy to a double agent.

Once in London, she was placed in solitary confinement and underwent long periods of interrogation by the experts of the Intelligence Service.

they seemed to be satisfied with her work, as shown by this extract taken from a top secret MI5 (British counter intelligence) memo, dated 26 May 1945: *"It is a rare thing to encounter so many lucky factors in this profession, especially when they concern any welcome exchanges with our French network: this is why, at this stage, that I deemed it fair that you know the high value that we place in BRUTUS and TREASURE."* (Letter from Denys Page, Assistant Director of the Government Code and Cypher School, to John Cecil Masterman, the man in charge of the system known as the Double Cross.)

Suspended by the Intelligence Service, Lily enlisted in the French army as a medic. Shortly afterwards, she married an American officer and left for the United States where she died in 1950 at the age of 38.

Despite the doubts raised by her behaviour in the days running up to D-Day, Lily Sergueiew's role in the successful of this particularly risky operation would appear to be significant. *"Lily was the most surprising main transmitting agent of the false intelligence campaign preceding D-Day that we know of to this day. It would be unfair to not state that her role was vital. She was the number one German agent and they placed a blind trust in her".* States Gilles Perrault, a D-Day specialist, in his postscript to Lily's account of this period where her personal problems intertwine with one of the great pages of history.

Lily seen her after D-Day in the uniform of a Free France officer, accompanied by her dog, Babs.

A secret American photograph showing anti-tank obstacles positioned on a French beach.

2. Alan Turing, the unsung hero of D-Day

A mathematician of genius, Alan Turing is seen as being the father of computing.

Not a single D-Day memoir, from Churchill to Eisenhower, or Montgomery, mentions Alan Turing, despite all of them knowing about the work undertaken by this genius concerning the deciphered messages that were received on a daily basis.

Alan Turing was born in London on 23 June 1912. He came to notice in 1936 via an article on mathematical logic that would become one of computing's cornerstones. At the beginning of the war, he was part of the research carried out at the top secret Bletchley Park trying to break the German *Enigma* code machines. His ground-breaking methods would allow for the breaking of enemy codes and thus decipher coded *Luftwaffe* (air force) and *Heer* (army) messages. Research to decipher the *Kriegsmarine* code machines would be more complicated.

However, the number of messages was such that it soon became imperative to create a machine capable of dealing with the multitude of incoming messages. It was Alan Turing who designed *Colossus*, a huge and complex machine that is considered as being the ancestor of the computer.

In 1943, Alan Turing went to the United States in order to work on spoken code and found himself involved in the work on the atomic bomb. After the war, he worked on one of the very first computers, then contributed, in a somewhat provocative manner, to the already loud debate on the capacity of machines to think.

Alan Turing, considered as being one of the greatest mathematicians of his time, came up with theories concerning artificial intelligence that are still classified and many researchers, here or there, continue to work on resolving them. According to several historians, he shortened the Nazi regime's ability to resist by two years.

In 1952, an affair concerning his homosexuality led to his prosecution. In order to avoid being sent to prison, he opted for chemical castration. Either by suicide or accident, Turing was found dead in his bedroom at his Manchester house on 7 June 1954, from cyanide poisoning.

At the request of mathematicians from all over the world, he was posthumously pardoned by Queen Elisabeth II in 2013. The following year saw an American-British film release called *Imitation Game*, about his life and especially the Second World War period.

A very late form of pardon for this unsung hero.

Colossus is considered to be the ancestor of the computer. It was designed at Bletchley Park by Alan Turing in order to decipher coded German messages.

3. How to kill time, on both sides of the Channel?

On both sides of the Channel, boredom was relieved in any way possible. In his tent in southern England, GI Humphrey tries not to think too much about what awaits him in Normandy. Once over there, the front-line will move so quickly that he will have to pack up his kit without having the time to take what is not essential, leaving behind his newspapers and games.

A game found in a young *Heer* (German army) soldier's billet in Caen, just after the first departures for the front-line. At an age where one dreams of girls, this soldier only had Panzers to kill time. Perhaps just before getting killed on a beach or between two hedges of the Normandy bocage...

4. Tiger, a tragic rehearsal that remained a secret for many years

It is one of the least known and most dramatic episodes of the D-Day preparations. At the end of April 1944, German fast attack craft wreaked carnage during an exercise off the coast of England.

As part of Exercise Tiger, these American soldiers take part in a live fire exercise on the beach of Slapton Sands, 25 April 1944.

One should always be careful with accountants, especially in wartime. In its Monday 7 August 1944 edition, the daily *Stars and Stripes* published an article concerning American casualties since 6 June. There was nothing surprising in this form of article given that it was the US Army's official newspaper in Europe.

The first paragraph spoke of German fast attack craft that had led to the deaths of 130 men and a further 312 missing, late April, during an attack on a convoy of GIs that was part of an exercise preparing for D-Day. These six apparently innocuous lines had the effect of a bombshell at the Supreme Headquarters of the Allied Expeditionary Force. Indeed, without knowing it, the diligent accountant had just revealed one of the best-kept secrets of Operation Overlord: the dramatic events that had taken place during the night of 27-28 April

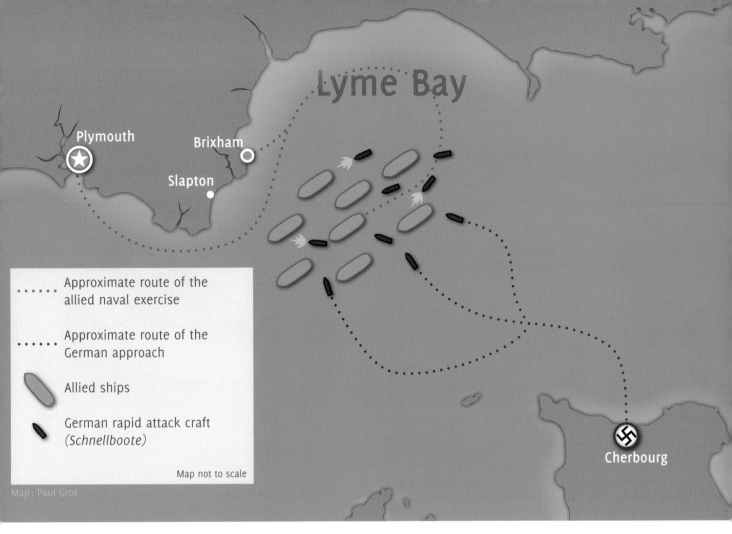

Lyme Bay

Plymouth

Brixham

Slapton

Cherbourg

...... Approximate route of the allied naval exercise

...... Approximate route of the German approach

Allied ships

German rapid attack craft (*Schnellboote*)

Map not to scale

Map: Paul Gros

off Slapton Sands in Devon. And even if these figures mentioned in the article are well under the actual casualty figures, the authorities went to any lengths to recover copies of the newspaper. This shows the importance that they attached to this tragedy, up to that point kept secret, in order to prevent it lowering the morale of hundreds of thousands of soldiers gathered in Great Britain awaiting the invasion.

Let us return to the night of 27-28 April 1944. Exercise Tiger was the third exercise in view of D-Day. Planned for a duration of three days, this large-scale exercise began on 25 April and involved no less than thirty thousand men and almost three hundred warships. During the previous winter, three thousand local inhabitants had been forced to leave their homes to make way for the military. The objective was a large-scale exercise for D-Day (with naval and air support and the use of live fire) in the bay at Slapton Sands, the beach of which was similar to that of Utah Beach, the most westerly of the zone planned for the Landings.

At the end of the day on 27 April, the German radars picked up the presence of enemy ships. At around 22.00 hrs, nine German rapid torpedo boats belonging to the 5th and 9th Flotillas, left Cherbourg and headed towards the allied fleet.

Using the thick fog, the *Schnellboote* attacked, in the first minutes of 28 April, a convoy of eight LST troop carriers (Landing Ship Tank), spread out over a distance of approximately eight kilometres. The convoy was initially escorted by two British warships, *HMS Scimitar* and the corvette *Azalea*. However, shortly after its departure, *HMS Scimitar* was forced to turn back to port following a collision.

The first salvo failed and no torpedo hit its target. However, during the second pass, the *Schnellboote* scored bullseyes against several ships. Hit in its engine room, LST 507 caught fire and this rapidly spread uncontrollably, forcing the captain to order to abandon ship. LST 531 was also hit by two torpedoes and also caught fire. After having alerted the rest of

In the early hours of 28 April 1944, nine German rapid attack torpedo craft from Cherbourg, attacked a convoy of eight American landing craft off the coast of Slapton Sands (Devon) that were taking part in Exercise Tiger.

Above: german torpedo boats in the port of Cherbourg.

Opposite: the *Kriegsmarine* rapid attack craft badge (*Schnellboot-Kriegsabzeichen*). (Fonds Fantastic Attic, Bayeux)

the convoy, the captain ordered the ship to be abandoned, before the landing craft capsized and sank.

The convoy broke up and zigzagged in an attempt to escape from the attackers that it could not see. The order was given to concentrate fire on the radar echoes. LST 496 opened fire by mistake on LST 511, causing several casualties. There was total confusion due to the darkness, fog, speed and low profiles of the German ships, that some allied sailors thought were submarines.

LST 289 opened fire on a *Schnellboot* that had just launched its torpedoes. Despite trying to avoid them, the enemy torpedoes hit the troop transport aft, pulverising the 40 mm gun and twisting the superstructure. The fires were got

Above: a German rapid torpedo boat. Length: 35 metres. Speed: 38.5 knots. Crew: 21 men. Armament: two 533 mm torpedo launch tubes with two reloading chambers (a total of 4 torpedoes), one 20 mm anti-aircraft gun at the bow, two 20 mm anti-aircraft guns in the middle and one 37 mm gun aft.

under control, but the rudder was damaged and the engine out of action. The LST launched five landing craft and its crews. The sixth was too damaged to be launched. Severely damaged, LST 289 nevertheless managed to limp back to the port of Dartmouth.

At around 03.00 hrs, the German ships, out of torpedoes, returned to Cherbourg. It was at approximately 05.00 hrs that the surviving ships reached Portland.

In all, 749 allied personnel (198 sailors and 551 infantrymen) lost their lives in the space of fifteen minutes and there were many more missing, 500 men were also wounded. The total casualty figures for Exercise Tiger reach 946. One can put forward several reasons as an explanation for such heavy losses. Survivors stated that some officers panicked and had ordered their men to jump overboard without any form of organization before the order was given to abandon ship. Eye witness accounts also show a defective inflation system for the life jackets and the fact that no demonstration as to their use had been given. Finally, one needs to take into account the long wait for help to arrive.

In order to keep it a secret, the allied high command immediately ordered the survivors to be kept in camp and under guard. Civilian doctors were kept away and the wounded only treated by military doctors who had to swear to secrecy. As for the families of the dead, they were notified without any form of explanation. Direct witnesses to the drama were threatened with court martial if they told anyone of what had just happened.

For the allied generals, the events were deadly serious, especially in light of the fact that ten American and British "Bigot" officers (those with knowledge of the impending invasion), had boarded the attacked ships carrying with them top secret maps of the Utah Beach sector. And, as luck would have it, these ten officers were amongst those listed as missing. They were no doubt dead, but had some of them perhaps been captured by the Germans? In the eyes of the allied supreme headquarters, there was, therefore, a chance that the enemy was in possession of the Operation Overlord plans. Therefore, Eisenhower ordered an immediate search for the missing that would only

LST 507 seen here before the attack by German E-Boats during which it was hit in the engine room, causing a fire that led to the craft being abandoned.

end when the ten "Bigot" corpses were found. They were all found eventually : the D-Day secret was safe and its final preparations could now go ahead.

The Tiger tragedy allowed the Allies to learn several important lessons in view of the Landings. In the short time that remained, they would have to notably improve radio system synchronisation between Americans and British, generalise the use of life jackets for the infantry, along with the essential training as to their use, and put into place efficient sea rescue procedures.

German torpedoes hit LST 289 at the stern, pulverising the starboard 40 mm gun and twisting the superstructure. Severely damaged, the craft nevertheless succeeded in reaching the port of Dartmouth.

THE STARS AND STRIPES

1D   Daily Newspaper of U.S. Armed Forces   in the European Theater of Operations   1Fr

Vol. 4 No. 237

New York, N.Y.—London, England—France

Monday, Aug. 7, 1944

Yanks Open Drive for Paris

Rivers Fail to Contain the Allied Flood

One Column 50 Mi. East of Avranches; Tanks Reach Brest

American troops started a double thrust toward Paris yesterday. It threatened to outflank the Germans facing British and Canadian forces in the Caen sector.

Driving eastward along two main highways to Paris, one U.S. column captured Mayenne, 50 miles east of Avranches, while another seized Laval, 17 miles southwest of Mayenne.

Some U.S. forces swung south at Laval and raced 17 miles to capture Chat-Gontier on the road to Angers.

Brittany was cut off by an American armored drive across the base of the peninsula to the Loire River near Nantes.

And the peninsula itself was virtually cut in half by an armored thrust into Brest, biggest French naval base on the Atlantic, after a record U.S. advance of nearly 100 miles in 24 hours.

The fall of Nantes was imminent last night. Lorient and St. Nazaire also were nearly within American grasp, as two other armored columns swept on toward them.

British troops cleared up the last German pockets in a 63-mile area near the west bank of the Orne River, after occupying Villers-Bocage, Aunay and Thury-Harcourt. The British held a nine-mi...

Reds 40 Miles From Cracow; Menace Silesia

Tighten Vise on Warsaw; Russians Still at Edge Of East Prussia

New retreats on the Eastern Front were admitted by Berlin yesterday as the Russians pressed to the edge of East Prussia, tightened their vise on eastern Warsaw and pushed within 40 miles of Cracow, Poland's second city...

said that RDX's tremendous blast effect makes a smaller bomb do as much

(Continued on page 2)

cover a retreat in other sectors. Vire was heavily bombarded by Allied artillery,

(Continued on page 2)

U.S. Toll in France Is 70,009; 116,148 Total Allied Casualties

German E-boats attacked a convoy of U.S. troops "during pre-invasion exercises the latter part of April," SHAEF disclosed over the weekend, with the result that 130 men were killed and 41 wounded, with 312 missing.

Word of the attack was made public for the first time, without any details, in a report listing these among 116,148 Allied casualties suffered in the French operations to July 20.

American losses were 70,009—11,156 killed, 52,710 wounded and 6,143 missing. British casualties were 39,594—5,646 killed, 27,766 wounded and 6,182 missing. Canadian casualties numbered 6,545—919 killed, 4,354 wounded and 1,272 missing.

The casualties were 30 per cent less than anticipated and only about three per cent of all casualties were fatal, said Maj. Gen. H. W. Kenner, chief medical officer at SHAEF.

Once a wounded soldier is moved across the Channel to hospitals in England, Kenner said, he has better than a 99-out-of-100 chance of surviving.

The combination of the medical man in the front line, jeep transport to advanced hospitals and air evacuation to Britain and the U.S. brings most of the Allied wounded under constant medical care within a few minutes after they become casualties.

Every week hundreds of U.S. soldiers

(Continued on page 2)

The tragic events of this exercise remained a secret for more than thirty years. It was only in the 1970s that a memorial was erected at Slapton Sands. In 1984, a Sherman tank that had sunk during the night of 27-28 1944, was recovered from the Channel and placed as a memorial to the events that took place.

IN MEMORY OF THE 946 AMERICAN SERVICEMEN WHO DIED IN THE NIGHT OF 27 APRIL 1944 OFF THE COAST OF SLAPTON SANDS (G.B.) DURING "EXERCISE TIGER" THE REHEARSALS FOR THE D-DAY LANDING ON UTAH BEACH.

À LA MÉMOIRE DES 946 MILITAIRES AMÉRICAINS QUI ONT ÉTÉ TUÉS DANS LA NUIT DU 27 AU 28 AVRIL 1944 DEVANT LA CÔTE DE SLAPTON SANDS (R.U.) PENDANT L'ENTRAINEMENT "EXERCICE TIGRE" EN VUE DU DÉBARQUEMENT SUR UTAH BEACH, LE JOUR J.

5 Juin 2012 l'association "Deep Respect"

Above: the allied headquarters issued orders that the events of Slapton Sands remain secret in order to prevent a negative impact on the morale of thousands of soldiers training for D-Day.

A memorial plaque at Utah Beach on memory of the victims of Exercise Tiger.

5. Force R, His Majesty's invisible soldiers

If ever there was a little-known allied unit, even to this day, it is that of Force R. Created in order to fool the enemy as far as the battlefield itself, it landed in great secrecy as early as D-Day.

Almost all of us know about Fortitude, the large-scale deception operation that was put into place by the allied high command in order to fool the Germans into believing that the Landings would take place in the Pas-de-Calais where the distance between France and England was the shortest.

On the other hand, who knows that Force R, created as part of Fortitude, secretly landed in Normandy as early as the evening of 6 June, equipped with fake inflatable tanks, optical sound speakers, small armoured vehicles and other special transmitters? Capable of producing the sound of moving tanks audible at over 20 kilometres, this very different unit would notably contribute towards fooling enemy armoured units and thus assisting the allied advance.

A special unit means special recruits. The Force R members all came from very diverse British Army units: Royal Engineers, Royal Electrical & Mechanical Engineers, Royal Corps of Signal, Intelligence Corps, Royal Signals. There were also architects and artists specialised in the painting of theatre backdrops.

The Force R headquarters was based in Colombiers-sur-Seulles, in a house overlooking the river and the village public washing space.

The Force R patch. The letter R was chosen in order to make it appear that it had been created as a reconnaissance unit.

Force R used fake inflatable tanks, as well as other means of deception.

Once deflated, the fake tank took up little space and only required two men to carry it.

This was the residence of Major Papillon, its commander and theatrical scenery designer in civilian life.

In the April 1994 edition of the Royal Engineers Journal, Lieutenant-Colonel Curtis details the role played by the unit fifty years earlier when, on 25 and 26 June 1944, sound simulators were used to make the enemy believe that a column of tanks was heading towards the front-line near Ranville. Thanks to the deciphering of enemy communications, the Allies discovered that this phoney information had indeed been believed by the Germans.

Invisible to the enemy, this unit nevertheless played a vital role in the success of the expeditionary forces led by General Eisenhower. It has left a visible trace of its actions in Normandy. Indeed, it was the Royal Engineers of Force R who erected the tall sculpture mounted with the god Eros at the crossroads known as "*Piccadilly Circus*" at Tierceville (Calvados).

The statue bears the inscription *"179 Special Field Royal Engineers. 23/08/44"*. Sober and somewhat enigmatic words, just like Force R.

The only real evidence of Force R's presence in Normandy: this tall sculpture mounted with a statue of the god Eros, was inspired by the one at "Piccadilly Circus" in London. It can be seen in the village of Tierceville (Calvados).

6. French Commandos dropped over Brittany

It was not only American and British parachutists that jumped during the early hours of D-Day. Thirty-six French SAS Commandos were dropped over Brittany in order to link up with the Resistance.

The objectives of the two French SAS groups during the night of 5-6 June 1944.

As the men of the American 82nd and 101st Airborne Divisions and those of the British 6th Airborne Division prepared to jump over Normandy, during the night of 5-6 June 1944, another drop over France was being prepared, one that was much smaller, but just as risky. Thirty-six French Commandos, in two four-engined Short Stirling aircraft, were flying towards Brittany. They were members of the Special Air Service (SAS), a British special forces unit created in July 1941 and whose motto was "who dares wins". Their technique was one of hit and run, literally hitting fast, leaving quickly and starting again a few kilometres away.

The mission of the French SAS was of vital importance : to coordinate and train the Resistance that was very active in this part of France, in order to prevent the Germans stationed there from reinforcing troops already positioned on the coast or nearby. The thirty-six men who were to jump were the first of others due to arrive later; their task was to set up two permanent bases where the other men and materiel would arrive in the following days before starting guerrilla and sabotage operations. Samwest, in the Duhault forest (Côtes du Nord now known as Côtes d'Armor), was attributed to the sticks commanded by Lieutenants Botella and Deschamps; and Dingson, in the

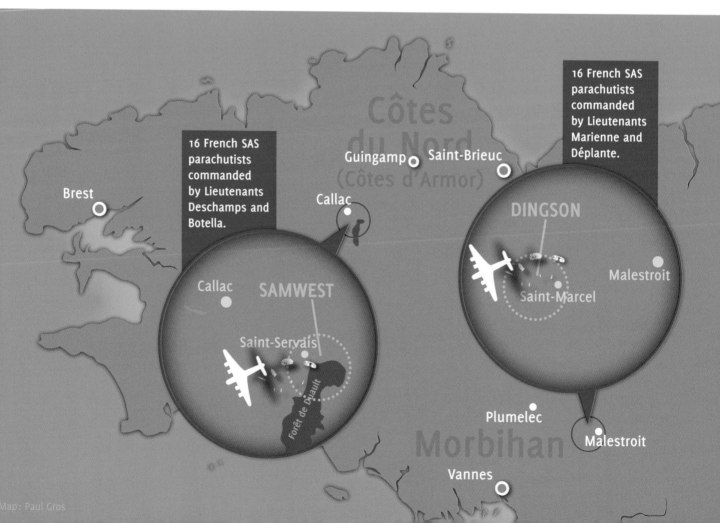

16 French SAS parachutists commanded by Lieutenants Deschamps and Botella.

16 French SAS parachutists commanded by Lieutenants Marienne and Déplante.

Côtes du Nord (Côtes d'Armor)

Guingamp
Saint-Brieuc
Brest
Callac
DINGSON
Callac
SAMWEST
Malestroit
Saint-Servais
Saint-Marcel
Forêt de Duhault
Plumelec
Morbihan
Malestroit
Vannes

Map: Paul Gros

Saint-Marcel forest (Morbihan), to the sticks of Lieutenants Déplante and Marienne.

Both groups were dropped just before midnight. The white canopies of Lieutenant Marienne's stick, who had not been dropped exactly where planned, were spotted by German soldiers posted on the Gree windmill on the high ground above Plumelec. The latter immediately alerted their superiors.

Once on the ground, Pierre Marienne led other SAS men in the hunt for the container holding the uniform of the officer who had jumped in civilian clothing in order to simplify establishing contact with the men of the Saint-Marcel maquis. *Caporal* Émile Bouétard was left at the drop zone to provide cover for the three radio operators and their equipment, Etrich, Jourdan and Sauvé, grouped together in a sunken lane.

It was then that the enemy attacked. In fact the latter were "*White Russians*", made up of Georgians and Ukrainians, who immediately opened fire. The attacking force was numerous and Bouétard, who returned fire with his Sten submachine-gun and by throwing grenades,

was soon under attack from all sides. He was wounded in the shoulder and thigh.

Just after his three comrades were captured, he was finished off with a burst of submachine-gun fire to the head. The following is what was written down concerning these events in the German army XXV corps war diary, the occupying force in Brittany at the time: "*At 01.30 hrs, French parachutists in English uniforms, tasked with sabotage missions, were taken prisoner by the East 285th cyclist group and taken to the army corps headquarters, then to the Vannes airfield.*"

The prisoners mentioned here are the group's three radio operators. As for Émile Bouétard, he died less than half an hour after touching the ground of his birthplace, Brittany. Aged 29, he was older than most of his brothers in arms. The son of farmers from the Côtes du Nord, he joined the French merchant navy at a young age. Mobilised as a sailor in 1939, the French defeat forced him to return home in the spring of 1940. Disgusted by the German occupation, he did everything he could in order to join De Gaulle. After an adventurous trip via Morocco

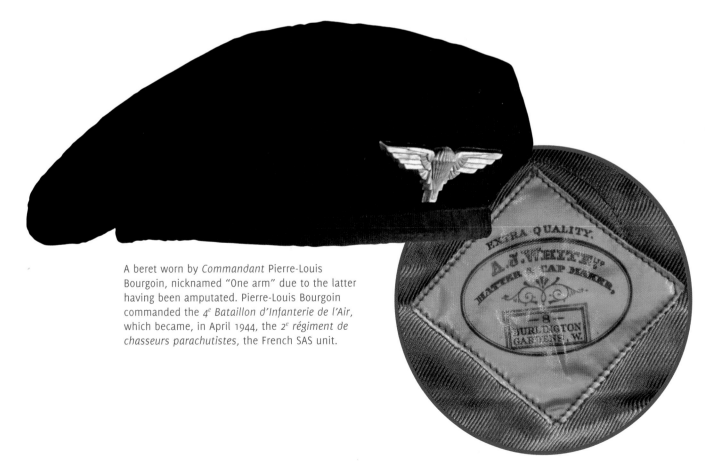

A beret worn by *Commandant* Pierre-Louis Bourgoin, nicknamed "One arm" due to the latter having been amputated. Pierre-Louis Bourgoin commanded the *4e Bataillon d'Infanterie de l'Air*, which became, in April 1944, the *2e régiment de chasseurs parachutistes*, the French SAS unit.

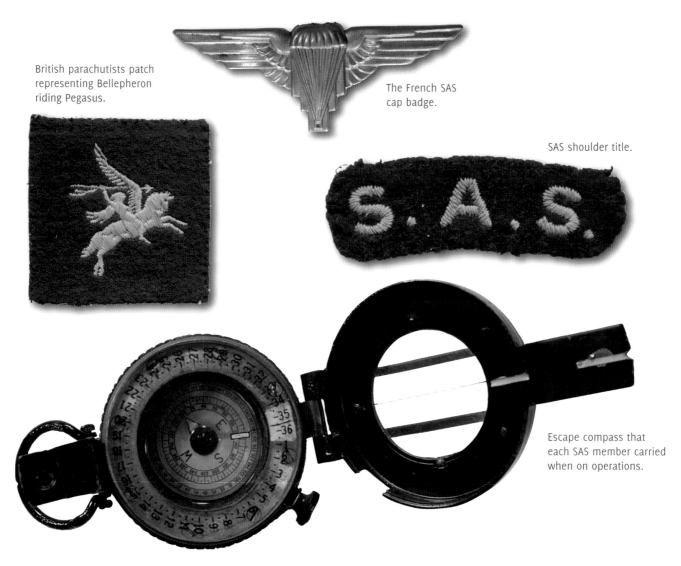

British parachutists patch representing Bellepheron riding Pegasus.

The French SAS cap badge.

SAS shoulder title.

S.A.S.

Escape compass that each SAS member carried when on operations.

and the United States, he finally arrived in England in January 1943 and joined, the following month, the SAS. Like his comrades, he underwent the tough and selective commando training in England and Scotland, making many parachute jumps, route marches through the countryside and close-quarter combat exercises. However, Bouétard, known as "old man" to the other men, got through the training, despite a shoulder injury. Nothing in the world would make him miss out from being amongst the first to be dropped over France.

The German report states that the three radio operators of the Marienne stick were taken prisoner at 01.30 hrs. This is German time which was one hour ahead of that used by the Allies and two ahead of the solar clock used by French farmers at the time. This is an important detail because Émile Bouétard is considered by some historians as being the first man to die during Operation Overlord. Other historians

believe that this sad privilege belongs to two British soldiers killed during the attack on the bridge at Bénouville on the eastern extremity of the Landings zone. We will not make any conclusions here. What is sure, on the other hand, is that *Caporal* Bouétard was definitely the first French soldier to die in the Liberation, killed several hours before the men of Commando Kieffer were cut down on the beach at Ouistreham at dawn of 6 June.

On 8 June 1980, a plaque in memory of Émile Bouétard was unveiled near to where the firefight took place at Plumelec. On the fiftieth anniversary of the Landings, a town square was renamed "*Place du caporal Émile Bouétard*" on 5 June 1994.

However, let us return to the night of D-Day. Still busy looking for the container, Marienne immediately decided to take his men towards the opposite direction from which the shooting and explosions were coming from.

He managed to make his way to Saint-Marcel where he found Henri Déplante and his entire stick. Further north, things had gone better for the sticks led by André Botella and Charles Deschamps. Dropped where they were supposed to be, they were able to quickly set up their base and go into action thanks to the small groups of maquis fighters that were hiding out in the forest.

In the following days and weeks, the strength of the French SAS in Brittany constantly increased and they were able to play a very active role alongside the Resistance until the region was liberated in August 1944, following the American breakthrough at Avranches.

Out of the 500 men who saw action, 77 were killed and 200 wounded. Amongst those killed was Pierre Marienne, Émile Bouétard's commanding officer, who was summarily executed with several of his men at dawn on 12 July 1944 at a farm in a hamlet near Plumelec.

Above: a group of French SAS. Several of the men wear the parachutists oversmock. *Caporal* Bouétard is in the second row, fourth from the left, recognisable by his small moustache.

Opposite: a parachutist's oversmock used by British airborne troops.

Killed in the Morbihan region less than half an hour after having touched the ground of Brittany, the land of his birth, *Caporal* Émile Bouétard was one of the first D-Day fatalities and the first French soldier to die in the Liberation.

Below: a tricolor pennant stained with blood, carried by *Caporal* Bouétard beneath his battle-dress during the night of 5-6 June 1944.

Below: 20 June 1944, French SAS with a maquis fighter in the Saint-Marcel sector (Morbihan).

LE 5 JUIN 1944 ICI EST TOMBÉ AU COMBAT
LE CAPORAL ÉMILE BOUÉTARD DU 2ᵐᵉ BCP
NÉ A PLEUDIHEN + C DUN +LE 4 SEPT ᵐᵉ 1915
PREMIER MORT DES TROUPES DÉBARQUÉES
POUR LA LIBÉRATION

7. The Allies come unstuck at the radar station

D-DAY
What we haven't told you...

A strategic part of the Atlantic Wall, the radar station at Douvres- la-Délivrande housed several *Luftwaffe* radars, one of which was a *Würzburg Riese*, a device that was at the forefront of technology at the time and capable of following an aircraft at a range of up to sixty kilometres thanks to its 7.5 metre diameter dish.

Completed in the autumn of 1943, the station covered just under 20 acres and was strongly fortified with bunkers, anti-tank guns, a 75 mm gun, numerous mortars and machine-guns, as well as minefields. Added to this was a six-metre high barbed wire perimeter fence. This veritable fortress was manned by some 230 *Luftwaffe* personnel, thirty of whom were air traffic controllers. It was linked to the nearby telephone exchange at Tailleville via underground cables.

During the night of 5-6 June, at around 23.00 hrs, the Allies started an intensive frequency jamming, rendering the whole German radar network blind between Cherbourg and Le Havre. On the morning of the 6th, the Douvres antennae were rendered unusable by air raids and naval bombardment.

However, this rapid neutralisation of its radar detection capabilities did not mean that the station had fallen. Far from it, in fact. First attacked by the Canadians that had landed at Juno Beach, then by British Royal Marines, the garrison held out heroically for several days and nights, awaiting a counter offensive due to be undertaken by the German 21st armoured division.

It was not until 17 June that a new attack by Royal Marines, supported by Centaur tanks, led to the capture of the Douvres-la-Délivrande radar station, more than ten days after the Landings.

For this decisive assault, the British soldiers received assistance from an unexpected, but precious source, in the shape of Jean Vallette, an architect from Saint-Aubin, who showed them how to cut off the water pipe supplying the entire station.

The remains of one of the antenna at the Douvres radar station, destroyed by allied naval guns on the morning of 6 June.

8 June 1944. After their first failed attack against the radar station, Royal Marines enter the town of Douvres-la-Délivrande.

8. Was there a Eureka beacon at the Bénouville château?

One hundred *Eureka* beacons were present in Normandy during the night of 5-6 June 1944.

This photo, taken a few days after 6 June 1944, shows Madame Léa Vion wearing an FFI armband, in the grounds of the Bénouville château that housed a maternity hospital at the time.

What if a *Eureka* beacon had guided the British parachutists who captured Pegasus Bridge over the Caen to the sea canal during the night of 5 to 6 June? There are some accounts that allow us to ask this question.

All over Normandy on that night, clandestine operators had been dropped by parachute shortly before the invasion in order to deploy *Eureka* beacons that would guide allied aircraft tasked with dropping parachutists or towing gliders. The Resistance also had this type of light transponder that worked along with a *Rebecca* (for Recognition Beacon) transceiver placed in the aircraft. The same device was also present on board two X Craft midget submarines positioned off the landing beaches of the British zone. In all, one hundred *Eureka* beacons were used during the night of D-Day.

Accounts also relate that a beacon of this type was used in the Bénouville château in order to guide the planes towing the British parachutists of 6th Airborne Division, tasked with capturing the bridge (Pegasus Bridge) over the Caen to the sea canal and the river Orne. This would not be surprising given that the Bénouville château was an important hub of resistance activity, thanks notably to its manageress, Madame Léa Vion, known as the Countess, who also had a radio transmitter. However, archive material does not show any sign of a *Eureka* beacon, but the question still deserves to be asked.

With a hundred *Eureka* beacons positioned in Normandy, would there not have been one at Bénouville, a place where such a thing would have been totally justified? All the more so given that the Allies had plenty of these devices at their disposal.

A positive answer to this question would take nothing away from audacity and success of the amazing assault that led to the capture of these two bridges that were of vital strategic importance to the Allies. This merely adds an extra element to the history of this brilliant feat of arms that will always be associated with the name of Pegasus Bridge.

Espionage at the Gondrée café

It would be surprising that in a place so well-known to the British intelligence services, that the Bénouville château did not have a *Eureka* beacon. Indeed, in 1935, the bridge at Bénouville had witnessed the testing, in 1935, of a French destroyer, Le Terrible, built at the nearby shipyards at Blainville. This 100,000 HP ship had come to the attention of the Royal Navy Admiralty due to the fact that it had beaten the world speed record of 45.029 knots. Indeed, it was at the Gondrée café, next to the bridge, that the Intelligence Service agents listened to the conversation of the Normandy shipbuilders, trying to pick up any snippets of information that might reveal the reason of the destroyer's amazing performances. Note that this speed record was not beaten by a ship of the same class until 2011... some 76 years later!

The landing of Major Howard's three gliders, grouped together near the Bénouville Bridge that would later be called Pegasus Bridge. This was an outstanding exploit, but was it helped by *Eureka* beacons? In this painting, we see the arrival of the glider N°3. It was 00.18 hrs and it would be a very hard landing. (Detail of a painting exhibited in Mémorial Pegasus.)

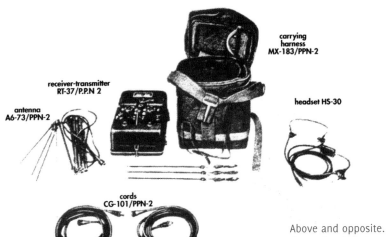

carrying harness MX-183/PPN-2

receiver-transmitter RT-37/P.P.N 2

antenna A6-73/PPN-2

headset HS-30

cords CG-101/PPN-2

Above and opposite. Created and designed by the British but made by the US Army especially for D-Day, these devices had remained a secret up to that point. It worked by sending radio frequency impulses between the planes, equipped with the "Rebecca" device (transceiver) and the "Eureka" (transponder) which guided the plane, with great accuracy, towards the desired zone. The devices only worked if the plane received the transponding impulses according to a code that was only known by the plane.

émetteur récepteur «REBECCA»

envoi d'ondes interrogatives à environ 2,4 km de distance

impulsions de réponse de la balise

Balise «EUREKA»

1/ "Rebecca" transceiver.
2/ Radio frequency waves sent at a distance of roughly 2.4 km.
3/ Beacon transponder impulses.
4/ "Eureka" beacon.

9. Comanche "Code Talkers" at Utah Beach

In order to encrypt their transmissions, the Germans had at their disposal the *Enigma* machine. On D-Day, at Utah Beach, the Americans had Comanche Code Talkers who would use their native language in the midst of the fighting.

Comanche Code Talkers at Fort Benning in 1941. In the foreground, Charles Chibitty and Simmons Parker wear traditional clothing.

Native American Indians played a bigger role than is thought towards the American war effort. Out of a population of 400,000, 40,000 of them saw military service. In very detailed book on the subject, *Sur le sentier de la guerre, les Indiens d'Amérique dans la guerre, 1939-1945* (éditions Heimdal, 2012), Stéphane Jaquet states that:

"No other minority contributed so much to the Second World War. From Normandy to the Pacific, via North Africa, Italy and the Ardennes, the soldiers from the Native American tribes showed, as they had in the past, a patriotism and courage that were rarely equalled by their white compatriots".

The 2002 film *Windtalkers*, brought the Navajo Code Talkers role in the Pacific theatre to the wider public. As well as being based on true events, the film, directed by Nicolas Cage, also pays homage to the Native Americans in their role of encrypting messages on the battlefield.

However, we know less of the fact that other Code Talkers played a role during the Second World War. This was a small group of Comanche men who had landed with the 4th Infantry Division (United States) at Utah Beach at dawn on 6 June 1944. Just like the Navajos at Saipan, they used a code comprising of words from their vernacular language in order to render messages between the front-line and the command centres incomprehensible to German listening stations.

Utah Beach, 6 June 1944. American assault troops land opposite the dwelling known as "the red house", a good point of reference when arriving from the sea. Amongst these soldiers are the Code Talkers of the 4th Signal Company.

This little-known story began at the beginning of 1941 with the arrival of seventeen young men from Comanche tribes at Fort Benning in Georgia. They had been recruited to form a Code Talker unit using their language which, at the time, was not written. The code would be made by the Native Americans themselves with the collaboration of 2nd Lt. Hugh Foster, the commanding officer of the 4th Signal Company, the signals unit of the 4th Infantry Division that would land at Utah Beach three years later.

They had to invent numerous military words that did not exist in the Comanche language. In order to do this, Hugh Foster gave the Comanche men an English word and they in turn would give a translation. Thus, tank became *wakaree'e* (turtle), a parachutist *pohpituu eka-sahpana* (jumping soldier) and bazooka *ek-sahpana piatawo'i* (big gun for soldier). They even made a name for Hitler: *po'sa taiboo'* (crazy white man).

On D-Day, the first message sent from Utah Beach was from a Comanche Code Talker: "*Tsa aku nunnuwee* (the landings are going

well). *Atahtu nunnuwee* (we have landed at the wrong place)". Indeed, due to a navigational error due to the strong sea current, the first assault waves landed almost two kilometres south of where the landings had been planned. This did not stop Utah Beach from being the least costly in human lives out of the five beaches.

As for the Comanche Code Talkers, they carried out their task successfully, carrying on until the end of the war and all returning home alive. Forgotten by history for many years, the French government made them all knights of the national order of merit in 1989.

Much later, in 2013, the United States awarded 17 of their veterans with the Congressional Gold Medal, the highest American civilian award. This was awarded posthumously as the squad's last survivor, Charles Chibitty, had died in 2005. Three years before his death, he said: "*It's funny, but as a child I had been forbidden to speak my mother tongue at infants school. Later on, my country asked me to speak it. My language helped win the war and that makes me feel very proud.*"

A short while after landing at Utah Beach, four soldiers of the 4th Signal Company have set up radio equipment in a shell hole. In the background, to the right, we can see one of the Comanche Code Talkers using his walkie-talkie.

10. Two little submarines that played a big role

Forgotten by history, the two X 20 and X 23 midget submarines played a vital role during the night of D-Day, that of guiding the ships to the three beaches under British command.

The British Admiralty had come up with an ingenious idea to ensure landings that would be as perfect as possible on the three beaches placed under its authority, Gold, Juno and Sword: marking the extremities of the zone with two X Class midget submarines, each equipped with a green light, radio beacon and echo sounder. The code

Twenty X Class midget submarines were built. Fifteen metres in length, they carried a three-man crew. The latter was increased to five for D-Day.

name of was Operation Gambit. The American high command had turned down the offer for the same operation at their two beaches of Utah and Omaha, something that would not be without consequences.

Designed for a three-man crew, these midget submarines were fifteen metres in length and only twenty were made, making their debut in 1942. For this new type of mission, they carried an extra two men: a positioning specialist and another for signals. It goes without saying that the air soon became unbreathable in the 2.5 metre long and 1.6 metre wide compartment.

The two "markers" arrived off the Normandy coast at dawn on 4 June (D-Day had initially been planned for the 5th), escorted by an accompanying vessel. They dived under the sea and settled on the seabed awaiting orders, X 23 (commanded by Lieutenant Honour) off Ouistreham and X 20 (commanded by Lieutenant Hudspeth) off Asnelles, just next to Arromanches.

During the night of 4-5, they surfaced in order to "take some air" and to observe the coast. After the war, George Honour said that: *"It was a delight for us to spot our waymarks: church spires, public buildings, the Ouistreham lighthouse... And even people on the beach with our infrared camera. It was then that we learned the Landings had been postponed. We would have to wait until the next day. If by any chance there would be a new postponement, given that our autonomy was for five days, we would have to scuttle and reach the shore with our civilian clothing and false identity cards."*

During the night of 5-6 June, the two submarines received the order to deploy their radio beacon antennae and 5.5 metre-high telescopic light mast, in order to guide the ships heading towards Gold, Juno and Sword. At 05.06 hrs, the D-Day signal light was raised.

At 09.35 hrs, George Honour sent his end of mission report to HMS Largs, the Force S flag ship. As was the case with X 20, the crew had just carried out a tough and exhausting mission over 72 hours, 64 of which were submersed.

Relieved at not having failed, Lieutenant Honour still felt a pang of nostalgia: D-Day was over for him, whereas for thousands of others it was just beginning...

Their job over, the two midget submarines now had to make their way through the landing craft and other vessels in order to reach the high sea and the trawlers that were tasked with taking them back to England.

A frogman equipped with Davis Submarine Escape Apparatus, on board an X Class midget submarine.

Opposite: crews were increased from 3 to 5 for D-Day.

The last surviving X Class submarine can be seen at the Royal Navy Submarine Museum in Gosport.

11. Ten navigation channels for the biggest armada of all time

In order to funnel some six thousand ships across the Channel, the allied planners had created ten navigation channels that were cleared of mines and marked only a few hours before the start of the operation.

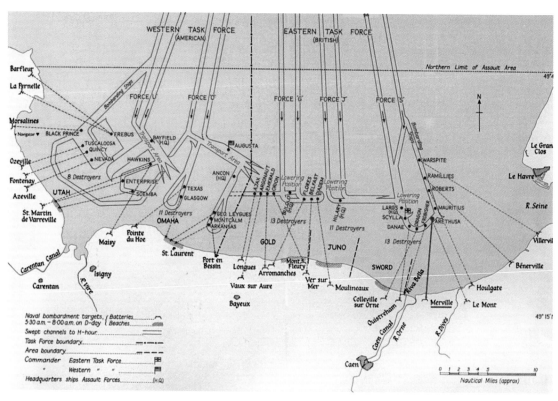

A map of Operation Neptune, with the positions of the ten navigation channels.

Some six thousand ships of all types sailed at the same time and in the same direction, but at various speeds, something that was not without risk, especially given the fact that it took place in wartime and that most of the crossing was carried out at night...

Thus, the Neptune (naval phase of Operation Overlord) planners created ten navigation channels (two per landing beach) that began at the assembly zone situated south of the Isle of Wight and named "Piccadilly Circus" in reference to the famous London road junction... and its reputation for dense traffic.

At a width of 400 to 1,200 metres, these channels were marked by lit red and green buoys placed at distances varying from two to five nautical miles. Every captain was issued with a chart on which the passage times of each ship at various buoys were noted.

In order to keep this gigantic naval operation secret, unprecedented in military history, the channels were cleared of mines and marked only a few hours before the start of Neptune. Everything had been planned down to the smallest detail so that this particularly complex machinery would not come to a halt. Given the fact that the dredgers required a maximum speed of 7.5 knots to cut the chains of the sea mines and that the landing craft could not move at more than 5 knots, the time required by the mine sweepers to change the mechanical sweeps when the tidal currents changed was taken into account. This made up for the speed deficit of the landing craft loaded with men, tanks and various items of equipment.

The minesweepers and buoy laying ships were guided by the usual direction finding and also by the British H2S and American H2X radars carried on board planes.

Started during the afternoon of 5 June, the minesweeping was easier than expected. We can put forward two explanations: either the mines had drifted due to the bad weather, or the mines had drifted due to the bad weather, or there were a lot less than German propaganda had led them to believe...

The fact remains that the luminous buoys were laid on just in time and that later, all the captains that had used one of the ten channels stated that they had had the impression of sailing along one the most well-lit avenues in the world...

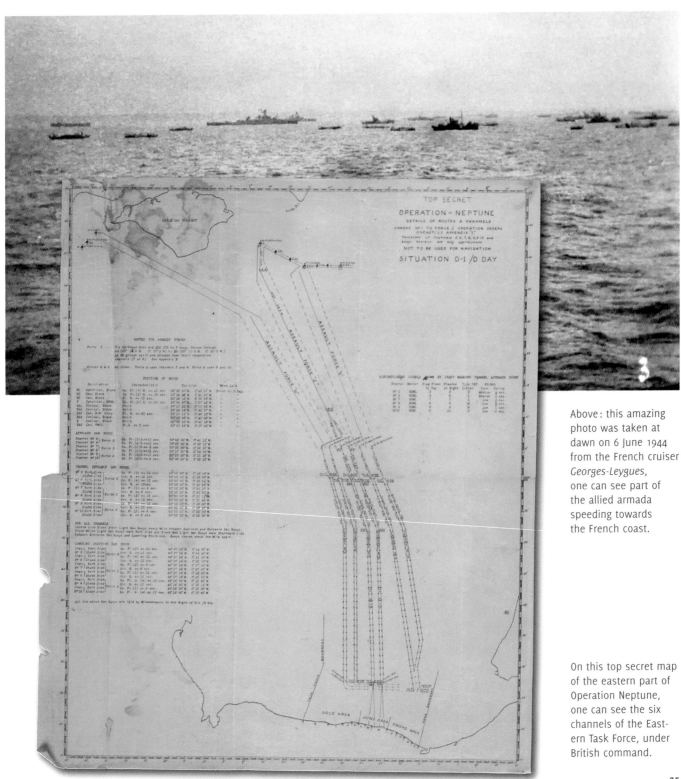

Above: this amazing photo was taken at dawn on 6 June 1944 from the French cruiser *Georges-Leygues*, one can see part of the allied armada speeding towards the French coast.

On this top secret map of the eastern part of Operation Neptune, one can see the six channels of the Eastern Task Force, under British command.

12. French pilots flying with the Allies on D-Day

Whether in fighter or bomber squadrons, French pilots played a vital role in air operations on D-Day. They would continue to fly ops throughout the entire Battle of Normandy.

It is less well-known that, as the 177 green berets of the Kieffer commandos prepared to land in the Ouistreham sector, other French military personnel were also taking part in the offensive. At sea there were sailors and ships of the Free French naval forces (FNFL). And in the sky, aviators were carrying out fighter or bomber missions. Out of the ten thousand aircraft that took part in Operation Overlord, one hundred were French. Although the majority belonged to units made up entirely of French personnel, a handful were integrated within Royal Air Force squadrons. All, however, shared the same special motivation and we can imagine the sense of excitement mixed with enthusiasm as they painted the black and white "invasion stripes" on the wings and fuselage of their aircraft.

At dawn on Tuesday 6 June 1944, the "Lorraine" Bomber Group (342 Squadron for the British) took part in Operation Smoke Screen which consisted of laying down a smoke screen that would protect the landing craft of the first American assault wave. As part of the thirty aircraft attributed to this role, six of the "Lorraine" Douglas Boston bombers would intervene in the sector between Pointe de Barfleur and the Saint-Marcouf islands, to the west of the landing zone.

Having taken off from England at approximately 05.00 hrs, the twin-engine aircraft, bearing the Cross of Lorraine, soon arrived over their objective. At an altitude that did not exceed fifty feet (15 metres), and flying at a speed of more than 400 km/h, they dropped their smoke

The insignia of the Free French Air Forces (FAFL).

Below: the "Île de France" Fighter Group, spring 1944.

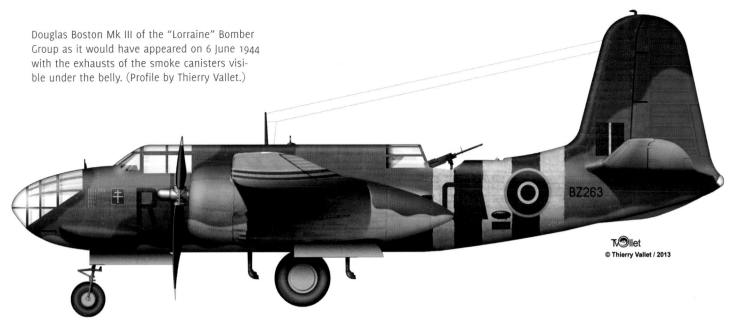

Douglas Boston Mk III of the "Lorraine" Bomber Group as it would have appeared on 6 June 1944 with the exhausts of the smoke canisters visible under the belly. (Profile by Thierry Vallet.)

canisters over the wavy sea. The sky was criss-crossed with the heavy fire of the German batteries. *"Each plane carried five canisters, each one took twelve seconds to empty, making a curtain of approximately three kilometres for each plane."* states François Robinard in his book *Les pilotes français du 6 juin 1944, les FAFL en Normandie* (Heimdal, 2013).

The mission was a success, but two aircraft had not returned to base with the others. One had been hit by flak and crash landed on an English beach. However, the other crashed into the sea near an American cruiser. Did it hit the sea? Was it shot down? We will probably never find out. What we can be sure of is that none of the three-man crew survived. At Utah Beach, there is a plaque to the memory of *Sergent* Boissieux (pilot), *Sous-Lieutenant* Canut (observer) and *Sergent* Henson (radio operator-machine gunner).

Other bombers flown by French pilots were also involved in D-Day and went into action a few hours earlier. These were the Handley Page Halifax bombers of the two Heavy Groups "Guyenne" (346 Squadron) and "Tunisie" (347 Squadron), which were not, strictly speaking, FAFL units but *France Combattante*. Both created before the war, these two groups were joined together in spring 1944 at the airfield of Ilvington, near York, in order to form Group 4 of Bomber Command. Combined, they had a total of thirty-two aircraft in two flights each with eight planes.

On D-Day, their objective was a network of bunkers at Maisy (today known as Grand-camp-Maisy) in the area between Omaha

and Utah Beaches. Positioned at the base of the Veys bay, this marshy area with clay bars, was impossible to capture for the landing troops. It was, however, of vital importance that it be neutralised before the invasion as its batteries constituted a serious threat for both American flanks. This is why the Halifax bombers of the "Guyenne" and "Tunisie" squadrons took turns, accompanied by British aircraft, in bombing the area between 23.30 and 05.15 hrs.

In all, 532 tonnes of bombs were dropped on that night on the Maisy batteries by all the planes that took part. A memorial was erected in Grandcamp-Maisy in memory of the actions of the two Heavy Groups in the hours preceding the Landings.

As the Halifax and Boston bombers were finishing their missions, the French fighters

For the D-Day operations, the planes were painted with black and white "Invasion Stripes" (A Spitfire can be seen here).

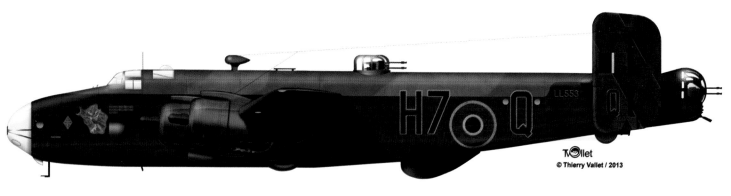

Handley Page Halifax Mk III of Bomber Group "Guyenne" (346 Squadron). (Profile by Thierry Vallet.)

took off from England. As early as daybreak, they flew cover missions to dissuade *Luftwaffe* intervention. These French fighter operations were carried out by the elegant and efficient Spitfire Mk IX of 145 Wing, known as the "Free French Wing" as three of its four squadrons were French: 329 Squadron (Fighter Group "Cigognes") commanded by Pierre Fleurquin, 340 Squadron (Fighter Group)"Île-de-France") commanded by Pierre Fournier and 341 Squadron (Fighter Group "Alsace") commanded by Christian Montet known as "Martel". On D-Day, these three squadrons flew a total of thirty-six planes. To this we must add 345 Squadron (Fighter Group "Berry").

Yves Ezanno, Squadron Leader of Royal Air Force 198 Squadron, seen here with his Hawker Typhoon fighter-bomber. (Profile by Jacques Clémentine.)

Finally, we must not forget the Free French flying within Royal Air Force squadrons. Led by the 32 year-old Breton, Squadron Leader Yves Ezanno, the Hawker Typhoons of 198 Squadron would attack the La Meauffe château north-east of Saint Lô, the headquarters of the German army's 84th corps.

In 602 Squadron "City of Glasgow", were the ace Pierre Clostermann, named as France's highest scoring fighter pilot after the war, Jacques Remlinger and Pierre Aubertin, commander of one of this squadron's flights.

Max Guedj, the son of a Casablancan lawyer, flew operations in his 248 Squadron De Havilland Mosquito. Philippe Livry-Level, approaching his 46th birthday (he took 14 years off his age in order to be allowed to fly) and father of five children, flew numerous operations over Normandy where he was born, as a navigator in a 21 Squadron Mosquito, once flying over his château at Andrieu, between Caen and Bayeux.

If ever there was a French pilot with reason to feel sorry for himself for not taking part in this historic day, then it is Jacques-Henri Schloesing. The son of an Alsace Protestant pastor, he had been promoted to command Fighter Group "Île-de-France" in September when he was not even 23 years-old. He had just returned to active service and had not yet been authorised to

The Spitfire Mk IX flown by French ace Pierre Clostermann (Profile by Jacques Clémentine.)

fly operations. Shot down over the Somme on 13 February 1943 and seriously burned, he had undergone several operations on his face. He would have to wait until 12 June before landing his plane in France (without his superiors knowing) on one of the campaign airstrips built by the Allies.

Jacques Joubert des Ouches would not be so lucky. Late morning on 6 June, his Fighter Group "Berry" Spitfire crashed into the sea a few kilometres from Saint-Vaast-la-Hougue whilst he was flying in the Utah Beach sector. A few minutes earlier he had radioed that he was having engine problems and he then bailed out at low altitude. He was 24 years-old. His dinghy was recovered empty, but his body was never found.

Jean Maridor would never fly to the land of his birth either. This 24 year-old from Le Havre was an intrepid and skilful 91 Squadron pilot and had specialised in shooting down V1 flying bombs. His technique against these flying bombs that the Germans had begun launching against England was efficient but incredibly risky. This consisted of flying as close as possible to the V1 and tipping it with a sudden movement of his wing.

However, on 3 August, he had been unable to tip a V1 that was heading towards a hospital. He flew at top speed behind the flying bomb

Pierre Clostermann, named at the end of the war as France's highest scoring ace, he flew a Spitfire Mk IX with 602 Squadron "City of Glasgow".

and machine-gunned it at point-blank range, leaving himself with no room to pull away if it blew up. Without any hesitation, he gave his life and his Spitfire disintegrated and crashed a short distance from the hospital that he had just saved. His death came one week before his planned wedding to a young English woman. His heroic gesture saw him become a posthumous hero in Great Britain.

French aviators continued to fly throughout the Battle of Normandy and on to the German capitulation. However, they suffered heavy losses.

From July 1944 to May 1945, nearly 80 Free French pilots were killed. As François Robinard states, *"With a death rate of 75%, the FAFL suffered casualties that surpassed any other allied unit or that they could have sustained."*

Jacques Joubert des Ouches disappeared at sea off Utah Beach on D-Day whilst flying his Fighter Group "Berry" Spitfire.

248 Squadron Mosquito flown by Max Guedj. (Profile by Thierry Vallet.)

© Thierry Vallet / 2013

Above: this high altitude photo was taken on 2 August 1944 by the German Arado 234 spy plane. The landing strip at Saint-Aubin-d'Arquenay, south of Ouistreham, is visible.

Above: a Royal Engineers soldier repairs a Horsa glider prior to it returning by air to England.

The forgotten airfield of Saint-Aubin-d'Arquenay

Specialist books talk of the fifty main airfields built in Normandy by the Allies in order to support the ground troops. However, they often overlook the smaller airstrips used by artillery observation aircraft such as the one near Bretteville-l'Orgueilleuse, or liaison airstrips set up near the various headquarters.

These airfields were coded "A" for the Americans and "B" for the British. This went from A-1 to A-29 and B-1 to B-22, with B-13 being left out (perhaps due to superstition) and that the airfields coded B-20 and B-22 were programmed but never built.

However, there is one that has been completely forgotten, even to this day: that of Saint-Aubin-d'Arquenay, south of Ouistreham. If the *Luftwaffe* photo analysts had not seen it on the photos taken at high altitude by the German Arado 234 jet spy plane on 2 August 1944, it would no doubt have disappeared into the mists of time...

Built by the Royal Engineers in a zone covered by gliders that had taken part in the invasion north-west of Pegasus Bridge, the Saint-Aubin-d'Arquenay airstrip's sole role was that of allowing repaired gliders to return to England and be able to take part in other operations. Therefore, no plane ever landed there. Each repaired glider had its tow cable stretched between two poles on each side of the runway and a tow plane snagged it in flight then took the glider back to England.

At each side of the runway there was a workshop for repairing gliders using parts that had been salvaged from various places.

A Horsa in position to be towed. It will be used again for Operation Market Garden in Holland.

13. The Invasion seen live

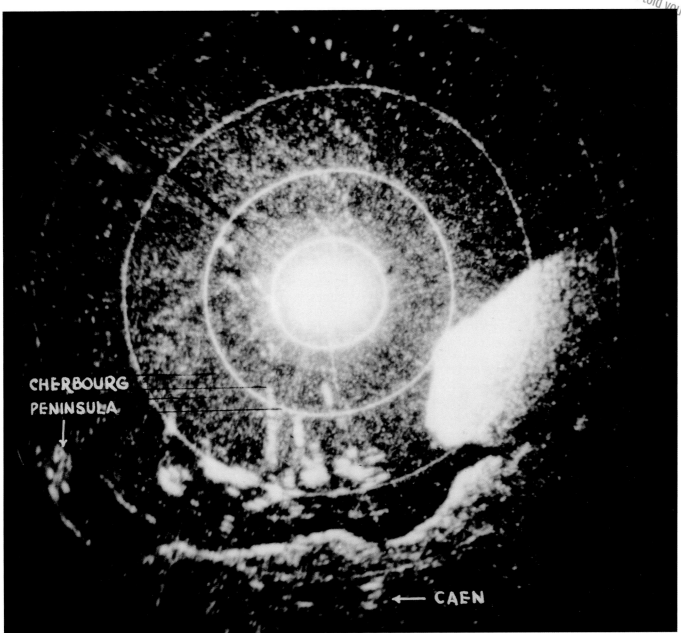

CHERBOURG
PENINSULA

← CAEN

This striking photograph, taken by an American bomber over the Channel, only a few minutes before the Landings, reveals the scale of the invasion fleet.

One can clearly make out the Normandy coastline, from Le Havre to the Cotentin, the Bay of the Seine, the Orne and the Vire.

Parallel to the coastline, one can see the radar echoes of the allied ships, battleships and destroyers in the firing positions off their targets. They were called Enterprise, Texas, Bulolo, Largs, Ramillies, Warspite, Rodney or Nelson.

Further to the north, in the three invasion channels leading the ships of the British Eastern Task Force towards Gold, Juno and Sword beaches, the radar echoes reveal a strong presence of vessels heading towards the coast. These are Forces G, J, and S. Each ship had a strict timetable for crossing the lit buoys that marked the predetermined channels. The strict adherence to these timetables was the only way to avoid jams amongst the six thousand-odd ships of all types in the zone.

14. The "Georges Leygues" scores a direct hit on the Longues-sur-Mer battery

There were a handful of French ships in the huge allied armada. One of these was the cruiser "Georges Leygues" which would play a decisive role in the knocking out of the formidable Longues-sur-Mer battery.

The Georges Leygues insignia.

A La Galissonnière class ship, as was the Montcalm, the Georges Leygues was launched in 1936. It was armed with nine 152 guns mounted in three triple turrets, eight 90 anti-aircraft guns, twenty-four 40 mm Bofors anti-aircraft guns in six four-barrelled mountings and 8 machine-guns.

Positioned between Omaha Beach and Gold Beach, the *Marineküstenbatterie* of Longues-sur-Mer was amongst the most formidable fortified positions of the entire Atlantic Wall.

The battery is at the top of a slight crest, approximately 450 metres from the shoreline, halfway between Port-en-Bessin in the west, and Arromanches in the east and eight kilometres north of Bayeux. It comprises of four

Regelbau M272 type casemates with two-metre thick reinforced concrete roofs and walls, positioned 300 metres to the rear of the small coastal cliff. Each of the casemates was armed with a 150 mm naval gun with an approximate range of 20,000 metres, which meant that they were capable of firing on ships at sea, be they warships or landing craft.

A fire command post, positioned 300 metres in front of the casemates, on the edge of the cliff,

Salve du cuirassé américain "Arkansas"

commanded the fire of the entire battery. It was equipped with the most up to date command system of the Normandy coastal batteries. As well as the casemates, only finished in May 1944, the site also had anti-aircraft protection consisting of three emplacements armed with 20 mm flak guns and, for ground defence, various small bunkers and a belt of barbed wire. Defensive trenches linked the various parts of the battery, allowing men to move around even when the guns were firing. The battery had a garrison of 180 men. Also, stationed a short distance away, an infantry battalion could reinforce defence in the event of a ground attack.

It was for all these reasons that the swiftest neutralisation of the Longues battery was of vital importance for the Allies. Thus, in the early hours of D-Day, the battery was the subject of intense air attack, before being subjected to a naval bombardment of equal ferocity.

The Longues-sur-Mer battery is the only site on the Normandy coastline where one can still see 150 mm guns in their casemate. This explains its great historical interest and why so many people visit it seventy years after.

At 05.30 hrs, the British cruiser, *HMS Ajax*, opened fire on the battery without causing any major damage. At approximately 06.00 hrs, the battery returned fire, targeting the *Bulolo*, the allied command ship for the Gold Beach sector, forcing it to change position. The *Ajax* and another Royal Navy cruiser, *HMS Argonaut*, drew closer and renewed firing on the German battery.

In these early morning hours of Tuesday 6 June, another ship began firing on the Longues battery. This was the *Georges Leygues*, part of the handful of warships representing the Free French Naval Forces (FNFL). Accompanied by the American cruiser *Arkansas* and another French cruiser of the same class, the *Montcalm*, it supported the difficult American landings at Omaha Beach, a place that would go down in history as "Bloody Omaha".

One of the 760 sailors on board the *Georges Leygues* was François Bellier from the town of Angers. Through the small porthole of his turret, this 26 year-old gunner saw hundreds of soldiers loaded onto landing craft sink. *"But there was nothing that we could do. It is a sight that I will never forget..."* He told us many years after.

François Bellier had kept a diary since enlisting in the French navy in 1937. Here is an extract from what he wrote down about the very first hours of Tuesday 6 June 1944. This is the eye witness account of someone who took part in, and saw, the biggest landing operation of all time.

"02.30 hrs we are 22 km off the coast. All night we see big explosions on the Cotentin coast and enemy flak. Allied aircraft carry out their biggest night bombardment up to now. Fires break out all over. We are all bursting to go.

03.00 hrs, combat positions. The guns are ready to open fire.

04.00 hrs, the enemy sends up flares to try and see our attack dispositions. No reaction from the German air force. We have absolute air superiority.

04.15 hrs. Huge fires break out. Flak guns are blown up, geysers of sand, thrown 150 metres into the air, are visible.

04.30 hrs, action stations. I go to my post in turret II, gun number 3 (triple turret with 150 mm guns). Captain Cornilleau, fire commander, comes to see us in the turret and gives final instructions. We are 8,000 metres off the coast, with the Montcalm and Arkansas battleship. We are at Omaha Beach.

05.20 hrs. The German concrete batteries open fire on us (approximately 155 mm calibre). The shells straddle us.

05.25 hrs. The Georges Leygues opens fire on the aforementioned batteries (Longues) and, thanks to its accurate fire, renders them silent.

05.50 hrs. Fire is halted (33 152 mm shells fired).

06.00 hrs. Fire resumes. The 90 mm guns bombard the beach.

06.30 hrs. Cease-fire. Fire resumes. 11 shells are fired on the German batteries at a distance of 5 km from the coast. The landing craft are beginning to land their first wave shock troops. Following our bombardment with our 90 and 152 mm guns, there are no enemy batteries left on the cliff tops between Port-en-Bessin and Vierville. The Longues has been destroyed by the Georges Leygues."

The following day, the Longues battery was subjected to a new RAF attack; at the end of the morning by a C Company of the 2nd Devonshire Regiment, falling easily as the will to fight of the enemy troops had been severely dented by the bombardment, the knocking out of one of the guns and the fact that they were cut-off from the rest of the German army. The remaining 120 men of the 180-man strong garrison surrendered.

As for the *Georges Leygues*, throughout the following days it supported the invasion operations, firing on other batteries, as well as on troop concentrations and armoured columns.

On Friday 9 June, a launch from the cruiser berthed in Port-en-Bessin, bringing in supplies to the town. The sailors received an amazing welcome and the French flag was raised on the church spire. The Free French sailors were presented with a bouquet of white roses which was then taken on board the ship and shared out. *"In our turret, a white rose stood out against the blood-coloured "fire" light. It was with joy that we smelt this soft scent that reminded us of our beloved France for whom we*

The *Georges Leygues* gunners gathered on the deck.

were fighting the Germans to the end" wrote François Bellier on this day.

The Germans would go on fighting for some time. Two months after D-Day, on 15 August 1944, the *Georges Leygues* was part of the naval force involved in Operation Dragoon, the landings in Provence. *"For us this was harder than Normandy. We were almost sunk by a large German coastal battery positioned at Saint-Mandrier, near Toulon. It was twinned with a small 40 mm gun which allowed it to find its range. A shell from this gun hit us on the stern deck. Men were killed. The Captain immediately ordered the ship to zigzag and laid down a smoke screen. It was this that saved us. Just after, a 380 mm shell landed in the wake where we had just been a few seconds earlier. This would have sunk the ship!"*

Fifteen years after D-Day, the battery of Longues-sur-Mer was used as the set of one of the most spectacular scenes of the film *The Longest Day*, released in 1962. It is in the command post that, under a hail of shell fire, that a German officer discovers with horror the endless lines of ships emerging from the mist as they head straight towards him.

Amongst these ships was the *Georges Leygues*, decommissioned in 1959 after having taken part in the Indochina war, then the Franco-British expedition to the Suez Canal in 1956.

As for François Bellier, he left the French navy in 1966 and died in 2012 at the age of 93 in the Anjou region, where he was born. In 1998, he had returned to Port-en-Bessin, where he was re-united with the girl, now a woman, who had presented the bouquet to the French sailors on 9 June 1944.

9 June 1944, the sailors of the *Georges Leygues* were presented with a bouquet of white roses by a young girl in Port-en-Bessin. François Bellier kept one of the petals in his diary until the day he died.

premières fleurs de France

Above: two months after D-Day, the *Georges Leygues* fired once more on German positions, this time during the landings in Provence.

15. After the assault, the bad surprise that awaited the Rangers at Pointe du Hoc

It was a costly and bitter victory for the Rangers led by Lieutenant-Colonel Rudder: the formidable 155 mm guns that they were tasked with destroying at the top of Pointe du Hoc had been removed shortly before D-Day.

The assault by the Rangers led by Lieutenant-Colonel James Rudder (a Texan farmer in civilian life) against the Pointe du Hoc, is one of the most famous episodes of the Landings. The film, *The Longest Day*, has immortalised the heroism of the 225 elite American soldiers who climbed up a thirty-metre high cliff under machine-gun fire and grenades, using ropes attached to grappling hooks and ladders supplied by the London Fire Brigade.

This rocky headland points into the sea halfway between Utah and Omaha Beaches and it was a vital objective for the D-Day planners. According to their intelligence, the German battery positioned at the top of the cliff was equipped with six formidable 155 mm guns (French made, 1917 type guns), which posed a direct threat to the troops that would have to land on Omaha Beach and also Utah Beach.

The mission went wrong from the outset. Due to a navigational mistake caused by sea currents, the landing craft carrying the Rangers landed at the foot of the cliff late by thirty minutes according to the set timetable. However, Rudder and his men nonetheless carried out their mission successfully. Within approximately a quarter of an hour, they were at the top of the Pointe du Hoc and were met with the sight of heavily cratered landscape that had been deserted by the Germans, except for a few snipers hidden in the numerous shell holes. The bunkers were there, some of which still had their guns showing, but there was not a single 155 mm gun to be seen. Following the intense air and naval bombardments, all of the guns had been removed and taken inland. According to the author and journalist Gilles Perrault, a specialist in D-Day history and its planning, the French Resistance had sent this vital information to London, but *"it is possible*

that the intelligence did not get there, or that it arrived too late." It is said that, in the days running up to the Landings, the guns were replaced with wooden poles in order to fool allied reconnaissance planes.

The Rangers climbed up the cliff using ropes equipped with grappling hooks and ladders supplied by the London Fire Brigade.

The Rangers defended
the Pointe du Hoc
until 8 June.

The Rangers take
two Germans and
Italian auxiliaries
prisoner, some of
whom are wearing
civilian clothing.

In any case, due to the non-arrival of reinforcements, the Rangers had to hold onto the captured ground for two days and nights, fending off several German counter-attacks. On the morning of 8 June, when relief at last arrived, there were only 90 combat fit men remaining.

Seventy years after, the attack on Pointe du Hoc still raises questions. We can ask, for example, why the attack went ahead given the fact that the Allied Expeditionary Force leaders, on board their command ships, must have seen that the battery was not firing. We should remember that the Operation Overlord headquarters had at its disposal two elite units tasked with seaborne attacks against German defences that had not been neutralised by aerial or naval bombardment.

To the east of the landing zone this were the Royal Marines of N° 46 Commando, led by Colonel Hardy, who had to be ready to go into action against batteries between Le Havre and Ouistreham. As was planned, this unit had been placed on alert on the morning of 6 June, in the Bay of the Seine river. As none of its potential targets proved to be particularly threatening, it was ordered to stand down. Thus, to their eternal regret the men of N° 6 Commando only landed on 7 June at Bernières-sur-Mer to

lend a hand to the Canadian troops that were experiencing difficulty in the area.

Thus we ask ourselves the question why if this had been possible for the British, why was it not the case for the unlucky Americans led by Lieutenant-Colonel Rudder? This question will have to be answered one day.

These aerial views of the Pointe du Hoc show more or less the same cratered landscape that was encountered by the Rangers of Lieutenant-Colonel Rudder on the morning of 6 June 1944. (Photos: Francis Cormon.)

16. The Luftwaffe was cruelly lacking in aircraft to tackle the Allies

On 6 June, the German air force was greatly outnumbered by its enemy. The reinforcements that arrived in the following days did nothing to improve the situation.

Focke Wulf 190 A-8 of *I./JG 26*.

It is an unquestionable fact: the D-Day planners gave it everything when it came to ensuring the most efficient air cover to the seaborne troops. For 6 June alone, the American 8th and 9th Army Air Forces and the British 2nd Tactical Air Force put together a force of more than ten-thousand bombers and fighters which, starting at daybreak, would hit the bunkers and other defences along the five beaches chosen for the Landings.

But what about the enemy counterpart, the *Luftwaffe*? The question is worthy of being raised as the wider public only has the images of the film, *The Longest Day*, to fall back on. In the latter, one sees *Oberstleutnant* Joseph Priller, commander of *Jagdgeschwader* 26 (26th fighter squadron), and his wingman, Heinz Wodarczyk, totally alone as they strafe at low altitude the British sector beaches on board their Focke Wulf 190, on the morning of 6 June.

This really happened. Taking off from Lille at 8 a.m., Priller and Wodarczyk were the first German pilots to encounter the allied troops. After having flown over Abbeville, Le Havre and the Orne estuary, they punched through the clouds at over 600 kph and only stayed over the beaches for a few minutes, before turning inland, no doubt leaving the landing British troops incredulous. Certain that they would not return, the two *Luftwaffe* pilots nevertheless got back safe and sound from this seemingly suicidal sortie, landing at Creil, the base of the *Stab* (headquarters) of *Jagdgeschwader 2 "Richthofen"*. However, as we will see, there were others.

This scene from the film alone sums up the inferiority of the *Luftwaffe* compared to the means engaged by its enemy in the first hours of the Landings. The numbers speak for themselves: more than 14,000 air sorties for the Allies on D-Day, compared to only 319 for the Germans. This makes a balance of power of 1 to 50 and, logically, minimal losses for the Allies, as is stated by Jean-Bernard Frappé, author of one of the leading books on the subject, *La Luftwaffe face au débarquement allié* (Heimdal, 1999): "*Half a dozen four-engine bombers and fifty fighters did not make it back to their bases in England, most of whom were shot down by flak, a few being shot down in chance encounters with Focke Wulf 190.*"

In view of an invasion, the German air forces in the West had a plan at their disposal "*Drohende Gefahr West*" (Imminent danger in the West). This plan was reviewed one last time at the beginning of 1944 and planned for the 24-hour transfer towards France, as soon as an invasion was announced, of as many units as possible. This was done in order to reinforce *Luftflotte 3*, a force that had been created as early as the summer of 1940 along the same Western Front. "*In order to deal with such a large air force, representing over one-thousand aircraft, the Germans had been making for months, and this in light of not knowing where the future landings would take place,*

more than a hundred airstrips, all positioned less than one-hundred kilometres from the coast and spread out between the Pas-de-Calais to Brittany", states Jean-Bernard Frappé.

On D-Day, only some of the *JG 2* and *JG 26* fighters were capable of intervening in Normandy. It was *JG 2* that flew the bulk of the sorties. At around 09.30 hrs, a dozen Focke Wulf, armed with rocket launchers, took off from Creil and headed for the coast. They

Josef Priller, the *Kommodore* of *JG 26*, seen here on the doorstep of his private residence, a caravan that followed him around the various airstrips used by his squadron.

Below: the Focke Wulf 190 A-8 flown by Josef Priller, *Kommodore* of *JG 26*, seen here as it would have appeared on 6 June 1944. It bears an ace of hearts along with his wife's name, "Jutta". The ace of hearts was the emblem of 6./JG 51, the first unit led by Josef Priller as early as 1939. (Profile: Thierry Vallet.)

Seen here at the Felds am Wagram airfield, late May 1944, these Messerschmitt 109 G-6 of *I./JG 27* will, in a few days' time, begin their long transfer taking them to France.

Ready for take-off, a Messerschmitt 109 G-6 of *II./JG 3*, armed with a 250 kg bomb. The *JG 3* fighters arrived as reinforcements as early as 7 June.

attacked the Gold Beach sector and lieutenant Wolfgang Fischer sank a troop transport ship. The *JG 2* pilots flew other sorties up to the end of the day, some of which were undertaken alongside *JG 26* pilots. It was the leader of *JG 2*, Major Kürt Bühligen, who scored the first *Luftwaffe* kill on the Normandy front, shooting down a P-47 Thunderbolt shortly before midday south of the Orne estuary. During the course of this same day, the men of *JG 2* added to their tally several other allied planes, Hawker Typhoons and P-51 Mustangs.

Following the sortie by their *Kommodore*, Josef Priller, other *JG 26* pilots took to the air, flying the bulk of their sorties at the end of the day. Shortly before 21.00 hrs, the Staffelführer of number 2 flight, shot down a P-51 Mustang south-east of Caen.

Large numbers of reinforcements began heading towards Normandy as early as 7 June: two-hundred extra fighters within the first 36 hours following D-Day, and a further 100 by 10 June. On this day, states Jean-Bernard Frappé, "*1,300 aircraft would be present in the*

West, of which 475 were fighters belonging to more than 20 groups which, in the meantime, moved in the worst possible conditions to the Normandy front."

On 26 June, the *Luftwaffe* had 529 fighters on the Normandy front and this number would reach its highest point of 581 on 20 August, Focke Wulf 190 and Messerschmitt 109 combined. Of course, these reinforcements changed the balance of power, but it remained clearly in favour of the Allies, going from 50 against to 1 versus 1 to 10 against 1.

However, as well as the omnipresence and numerical superiority of the Allied fighters, the *Luftwaffe* was faced with another problem that would affect its operational capability: the attacks preceding the Landings had severely damaged the conditions in which the newly arrived groups could establish themselves. All of this meant that, by the end of June, most of the units had *"mostly lost their offensive capability"*, as Jean-Bernard Frappé underlines.

"The Germans may have inflicted losses to the Allies, but proportionally they lost more aircraft. This situation sapped the Germans' morale who, mockingly stated that a grey plane was American, a black one British and an invisible one German", says Olivier Wieviorka in his book *Histoire du Débarquement en Normandie* (Le Seuil, 2007).

No longer enjoying air superiority the *Luftwaffe* could not protect the reinforcements (armoured and infantry divisions) being sent to the front-line. Thus, the 2nd Panzer, stationed in the Somme, only arrived in Normandy on 13 June and would only be operational a week later.

General der Jagdflieger (commander of the German fighter forces) Adolf Galland (centre), accompanied by Josef Priller (right) during the inspection of *JG 26* in the summer of 1944. On the right is fighter inspector Hannes Trautloft. This photo was taken in the first days following the Landings, in the gardens of the château of Villiers-le-Bâcle, close to the Guyancourt airfield.

17. A self-heating food tin

Below: one had to start by piercing the tin in the two places indicated by arrows.

Ver-sur-Mer, 6 June 1944. Given that it was particularly cold for the time of year, the hot chocolate milk is enjoyed by British soldiers, as well as these young Normandy boys, looking with wonder at this revolutionary invention.

O f all the innovations brought over by the Allies, this is certainly one of the most striking. Indeed, many Normans were surprised to be able to eat soup, drink tea, a vitamin drink or chocolate milk in the middle of a field without using something to heat it up.

There were various soups, but also vitamin drinks or chocolate milk.

It could be said that the self-heating tin is forever linked with the summer of 1944, as much as for the soldiers as for civilians. Its beginnings went back to 1942, when the British government asked the quartermaster services to design assault rations, but also find a way of heating a meal without using fire.

The companies of Heinz and Imperial Chemical Industries developed a revolutionary idea for the time: a tin with a central tube closed with a meal lid; inside the tube was combustible fuel with a wick. Everything had been thought of down to the last detail: once the tin was opened and the wick lit with a lighter, a match or just a cigarette, the fuel did not create a glow and thus remained invisible by day, or night.

The self-heating tin went into full-scale production beginning in March 1944. It would have its baptism of fire, if we can say it that way, during D-Day. Throughout the entire Battle of Normandy, the GIs and the Tommies were thus able to really enjoy (?) "turtle" (in fact made with veal giblets), tomato, chicken, oxtail or kidney soups.

18. A strange water soluble coffee

Following the stock exchange crash in the 1930s, Brazil found itself with a surplus of coffee, to such an extent that it had to burn it in the boilers of its locomotives. This led it to ask Nestlé to look into the making of water soluble instant powdered coffee. The first experiments were a disaster as the precious aromas were lost along the way. It was only in 1937 that Nestlé came up with a satisfactory product, named Nescafé. A little later, the Swiss company created Nestea. The launch of these two new brands was not unsuccessful.

It took the interest shown by the US Army, at the beginning of the war, to boost Nescafé. The GIs succeeded where Nestlé's salesmen had failed, hailing the virtues of the instant coffee in all the theatres of operations throughout the world.

From the very start of D-Day, the Normans discovered and enjoyed this unknown drink that would help forge links between the soldiers and the civilian population, with the GIs happily sharing their Nescafé. The Tommies did the same with their Nestea, albeit with the addition of powdered milk.

It is also said that the Americans gave sachets of Nescafé to Russian soldiers in Germany; the latter, not knowing how to use it, consumed it directly without adding water, something that led to the odd discomfort.

However, one should not see here the beginnings of the Cold War...

Nescafé helped forge links between the soldiers and the Normandy population.

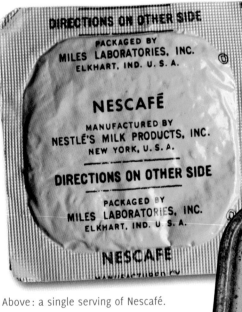

Above: a single serving of Nescafé.

The British had a preference for Nestea.

19. "Lili Marleen", the summer hit, both with the Germans and the Allies

The Germans called it "Lili Marleen", the Allies "Lilli Marlene".
However, the spelling is of little importance: this nostalgic
love song was enjoyed by the soldiers of both sides.

Above: there were several versions of the song, including that performed by the British Billy Cotton and His Band who played in France after the Liberation.

In this summer of 1944, the Normans were amazed to hear the through the headphones of allied armoured vehicles the BBC broadcasting the famous song of Lili Marleen, the same that had been hummed for years by the occupying troops. It has to be said that going from, in just a few days, *"Vor der Kaserne, Vor dem großen Tor, Stand eine Laterne"* to *"Underneath the lantern, by the barrack gate"* was somewhat surprising.

But it was this way, that the GIs and Tommies brought with them, as well as chocolate and chewing gum, this melancholy tune, the destiny of which was just as eventful as the story it told; that of a young love-struck German soldier as he is mobilised during the Great War.

Let us go back a few years. On 18 August 1941, British bombers destroyed the record warehouse of lieutenant Heinz-Karl Reitgen, head of the German military radio service in

The Normans were totally surprised to hear the allied tank crews listening to Lilli Marleen through their headphones.

Belgrade. For want of anything better, the officer in question decided to broadcast a song that, at the time, had been discarded: Lilli Marleen, inspired by a nostalgic love poem written in 1915 by the novelist Hans Leip, mobilised at the time, and recorded in 1938 by Lale Andersen with music by Norbert Schultze.

Deemed as being "dull and without rhythm" by critics when it came out, the song would soon encounter phenomenal success... almost worldwide. As Radio Belgrade was listened to from Norway to North Africa, Lilli Marleen won over not only Wehrmacht men struggling with the cold, but allied soldiers fighting in Tripolatania as well.

In the space of six months, the song was translated into almost fifty languages. In the spring of 1943, the British Army was forced to produce an English version after Goebbels had Lale Anderson record an English-adapted version in order to demoralise the Allies. The versions recorded by Anne Shelton and Vera Lynn encountered lightning success as soon as they came out.

The Americans made the most of the Liberation to take the rights to the song. The German-born American actress and singer, Marlene Dietrich, recorded a more languorous, but more energetic version in 1944. She went on to sing it during sixty concerts in Europe held for General Patton's 3rd US Army. Marlene Dietrich ended up making the song her own by modifying the words and renaming it with her name: Lily Marlene.

After the war, the song was forbidden in several dictatorships, on the grounds that it had been sung by both sides. It even became the anti-atomic anthem during the Cold War.

The English version song sheet.

Poster of the *Lili Marleen* film (1981) directed by Rainer Werner Fassbinder and inspired by the love affair between the song's first singer, Lale Andersen, and the Jewish composer Rolf Liebermann.

With their mission accomplished, French commandos chat with civilians.

This is why its capture was one of two missions given to the commandos led by Philippe Kieffer, along with the neutralisation of German defences positioned along the seafront.

The French green berets carried out these two tasks with bravery and efficiency, but at the cost of heavy losses. On the evening of 6 June, the sole French unit integrated into the invasion force had lost ten men killed and thirty wounded, almost a quarter of its strength. The capture of the casino bunker alone cost three men killed: Paul Rollin, the medical officer, Lion and Emile Renault.

Wounded in the leg on the beach, Philippe Kieffer refused to be taken away and remained at the head of his men in order to lead the attack on the casino bunker. In *The Longest Day*, we see him, played by the actor Christian Marquand, divert a tank and making head towards the objective. This scene really happened. By silencing the bunker's guns, as well as an artillery gun placed at the top of the viewing platform, on the other side of the

time when the only thing one risked losing was one's savings or fortune.

By observing aerial photographs that revealed its large surface area, the allied intelligence services, also intrigued by its flatness and lack of elevation, made it a priority objective for the troops due to go into action at Ouistreham.

Philippe Kieffer, leader of the *1er Bataillon de fusiliers marins commandos*, is decorated by General Montgomery, 16 July 1944.

avenue leading to the sea, this tank played a decisive role in the capture of this cornerstone of the German defensive system.

Despite its flaws, *The Longest Day* was met with great success when it came out in the autumn of 1962., with almost 12 million people seeing it in France alone. Each time it is shown on television it draws in a good audience. However, it no longer trips fuse boxes, as it did on an evening in 1976, when it was shown on television for the first time in France; so many television sets were on at the same time that the electricity grid could not cope and two regions suddenly lost the picture: Brittany and Normandy.

The Combined Operations patch, worn on the shoulder by all commandos.

Below: the green beret worn by commandos, with the distinctive badge worn by Kieffer's men, designed in early 1944 by *Caporal* Maurice Chauvet. The shield bears the Brig L'Aventure, the Commando dagger and the Cross of Lorraine.

The shoulder title worn by the men of the Franco-British N°4 Commando.

Commandant Kieffer was played by one of the French stars of the day, Christian Marquand (left), in the film, *The Longest Day*.

A Second Empire style building was built for the set of *The Longest Day* at Port-en-Bessin, at the foot of the Vauban tower. The scene depicting the casino attack required two weeks of shooting. It lasts for less than ten minutes in the three-hour film.

21. The Royal Navy's star diver in action on the Normandy coast

Lionel Crabb, the most famous British frogman, distinguished himself in Normandy in the days that followed the Landings. His fame owes as much to the success of his numerous perilous missions as it does to his numerous female conquests.

Lionel Crabb (centre) accompanied by two other explosives disposal divers Like his comrades, the Royal Navy Principal Diving Officer, is equipped with the Davis Submarine Escape Apparatus.

Born on 28 January 1909 into a poor family from south-west London, Lionel Kenneth Philip Crabb started out in life with a succession of small jobs. After two years at HMS Conway Naval College, he joined the Merchant Navy but joining at the same time the Royal Navy Volunteer Reserve. Having entered into active service in 1941, he was sent the following year to Gibraltar where he was posted to a unit tasked with neutralising limpet mines that the Italians stuck to the hulls of allied ships.

In 1942, The British Prime Minister, Winston Churchill, was so impressed by the repeated successes of the Italian combat frogmen that he urged the Royal Navy command to look into the subject. The British came up with the creation of three types of combat diver: manned torpedoes copied from those used by the Italians and named Chariot, Clearance Divers tasked with the demolition of sea obstacles before a landing and, finally, the divers of the Special Boat Section, equipped with kayaks.

Opposite: the Davis Submarine Escape Apparatus used by Lionel Crabb in Normandy, in 1944. Like the mask and fins, it was given to one of his numerous female admirers at Arromanches. In this photo, the apron designed to slow down the divers' ascent to the surface is deployed. (Photo Erik Groult-Heimdal.)

Above: a British post card printed during the war and showing a group of Royal Navy divers ready to enter the water equipped with the Davis Submarine Escape Apparatus.

The same device, this time with the flap rolled up and retained by a string tie. (Photo Erik Groult-Heimdal.)

At the beginning of his Gibraltar posting, Lionel Crabb was tasked with disarming mines that had been brought to the surface. He was not, however, totally happy with this work and decided, off his own bat, to learn how to dive and disarm mines at sea. Once he was operational, he joined a group of divers operating in the port against the attacks led by Italian combat frogmen.

In order to operate underwater without being seen, Crabb and his comrades used a new type of breathing device, the Davis Submarine Escape Apparatus. This closed-circuit device used pure oxygen. All of the air breathed out by the diver was recovered and passed via a soda lime filter that absorbed the carbon dioxide. As it was not equipped with a valve, it was silent and did not produce bubbles that could be seen on the surface: two essential and vital requisites for combat divers. "No bubbles, no noise",

as the British said in reference to this undetectable apparatus.

In view of D-Day, the Allies designed a variant of the Davis Submarine Escape Apparatus, specially studied for the crew of the amphibious Duplex-Drive tanks. Named the Tank Escape Apparatus, it passed more easily through a turret hatch but, above all, through the even narrower escape hatch. Indeed, the first tests carried out showed that a sinking tank had an annoying tendency to turn over due to the very heavy weight of the turret. Given that we know that the bulk of the D-D tanks would sink on 6 June 1944, we can say that the Davis Submarine Escape Apparatus saved many lives that day.

After having come to the fore in Gibraltar, then in Italy during the mine disposal in the ports of Livourne and Venice, Lieutenant commander Crabb, who had earned the nickname "Buster"

Lieutenant-Commander Lionel Crabb (left) coming out of the water at Arromanches in 1944. Both divers are equipped with the Davis Submarine Escape Apparatus.

in reference to the American actor and swimmer Buster Crabbe, was part of Operation Overlord. Along with the men of his Royal Navy underwater clearance unit, based in Arromanches, he undertook in Normandy numerous missions, notably following the gale of 19 June which destroyed one of the allied artificial harbours. Between his missions, where he risked his life each time, the star diver was a successful skirt chaser. Before returning to England, he gave all of his equipment to one of his numerous conquests.

He would also distinguish himself in the Caen sector, proving once again his courage and great dexterity during a particularly perilous mission. He dived on the wreck of the *Otto Bröhan*, a trawler armed by the *Kriegsmarine* and put into service with the *Vorposten-flottille* based at Saint-Malo. Before withdrawing, the Germans deliberately scuttled the fifty-five-metre long vessel in the Caen canal leading to the sea, opposite the Caen coal port. Also, they had mined the ship so that it would blow up if refloated, thus blocking the canal that led from the town to the sea.

Crabb managed to disarm the explosives. As for the trawler, once refloated, it was refurbished and started a new career as *I.H. Nicolas* (*Ingénieur Hydrographe Nicolas*).

Demobbed early 1948 with the rank of Lieutenant-Commander and the award of an Order of the British Empire, Lionel Crabb returned to civilian life, but remained with the Royal Navy Volunteer Reserve. At the beginning of the 1950s, he returned to active service within the Torpedo and Anti-Submarine Branch. He took part in trials of submarine equipment and rescue missions. It was in this capacity that he dived to inspect two sunken submarines, *HMS Truculent* and *HMS Affray*, in order to see if

The diving mask used by Lionel Crabb in Normandy in 1944.

Medium-size fins used by Lionel Crabb in Normandy.

Large-size fins used
by Lionel Crabb
in Normandy.

As was also the case for the writer Ian Fleming, heavy smoking and drinking had affected Crabb's health and he was, without dispute, no longer the invincible diver of the Second World War.

In January 1956, the Admiralty learned that several Soviet warships were due to arrive, between 18-27 April in Portsmouth, as part of a state visit by Nikita Khruschev and the Premier of the Soviet Union, Nikolai Boulganin. It was thus decided to use this occasion for a new underwater mission. This would be Operation Claret and Crabb would be the frogman.

In the early morning of 19 April, Crabb dived from HMS Deepwater to spy on the rudder and propellers on the Russian vessels. Encountering problems with his equipment, he had to turn back after twenty minutes. Following some adjustments carried out by his comrade Edward Davies, Crabb returned to the water. He had autonomy of two hours for a mission that was not to exceed sixty minutes.

He did not reappear. Soon, the British press got hold of the story, notably showing surprise that the pages of register of the Portsmouth hotel where Crabb and his team had stayed, had been ripped out for the period of 17 to 19 April. Theories then abounded in an attempt to explain the disappearance of the Second World War hero.

there were any survivors on board. Crabb's intervention was fruitful in both cases and only served to enhance his prestige which was already riding high in Great Britain. .

Having reached the age limit in 1955, Commander Crabb was forced to discard his uniform. He was not, however, finished with diving. On the contrary we might say, in light of what was awaiting him. At the end of this same year, the First Lord of the Admiralty, Lord Mountbatten, asked him, and without any trace of a written order, to take a look at the hull of a Soviet cruiser anchored in Portsmouth.

This operation having resulted in useful information regarding the superiority of USSR vessels in terms of manoeuvrability, Lionel Crabb was recruited by MI-6, the famous Secret Intelligence Service, employer of a certain James Bond, whose first adventures had been published in 1953 under the title of Casino Royale.

This guessing as to what happened grew further with the discovery, on 9 June 1957, of the body of a man the same size as Crabb, off Pilsey Island to the east of Portsmouth. The body was wearing the same diving suit as Crabb, but was headless and missing its hands. The impossibility of identifying the body led to the wildest rumours. It was said that Crabb had been taken prisoner by the KGB and was held in Moscow, and even that he now led a Soviet submarine unit with the Black Sea fleet, under the name of Lvovich Korablov…

Two theories are favoured today; either Crabb perished due to the wrong gas mix caused by his faulty equipment, or he fell victim to the Soviets. The latter is backed up by something that was said two days after Crabb's disappearance, by the Soviet rear-admiral Kotov, to the chief of staff of the Portsmouth naval command. Early in the morning of 19 April 1956, three Soviet sailors supposedly spotted Crabb reaching the surface. Shot at by two marksmen firing from the deck of a destroyer, the spotted man received a fatal head wound.

As for us, we rather think that the cause lies in a diving accident. Indeed, the Davis Submarine Escape Apparatus was a very tricky device to use. We also know that Crabb drank and smoked a lot. This is why, for us, it seems highly possible that he died in an accident and that the British authorities did everything they could to deny this explanation as a legend such as Lionel Crabb should remain intact.

What is certain is that sixty years after his disappearance, Lionel Crabb continues to fascinate historians. We also understand why Ian Fleming, a former member of the secret services during the war, drew inspiration from Crabb when he went from undertaking clandestine operations to the typewriter to add substance to 007.

Opposite: a diver equipped with the Davis Submarine Escape Apparatus, on board a British midget submarine.

This boat, the former trawler *Otto Bröhan*, had been fitted with mines by the Germans after being scuttled opposite the Caen coal port. This was done so that it would blow up when the Allies re-floated it, in the hope that it would block the canal leading from Caen to the sea. It was Crabb, who was based in Arromanches at the time, who dived on the wreck and defused the explosive devices.

22. The "Grand Bunker" at Ouistreham, captured... without a shot being fired

A strategic observation and command post, the "Grand Bunker" at Ouistreham was captured intact, three days after the Landings. Unlike the Casino bunker, it fell without any fighting.

Above: after two attempts to blow open the heavy armoured doors of the Grand Bunker, it took the British sappers four hours to penetrate the interior.

Lieutenant Bob Orrell captured the Grand Bunker on the evening of 9 June, taking the 53 occupants prisoner without firing a single shot. (Coll. © Grand Bunker.)

At the end of the day on 6 June, when the British and French Commandos left Ouistreham to take up positions on the right bank of the Orne, the town was in allied hands. At least, almost...

Indeed, one of the fortifications was still in the hands of the occupying forces. This was no ordinary bunker. It was the firing command post that was visible from very far away. At seventeen metres high, it allowed the Germans to watch over the Bay of the Seine river in an arc of fifty kilometres.

Its construction was carried out by the Organisation Todt and began in September 1943, with the bulk of the work being finished by mid-November of the same year. As for its equipment, it was only fitted out a short time before the Landings.

As well as an observation platform equipped with a range-finder, this four-floor building housed a command centre with a telephone switchboard, a radio room, technical installations, dormitories and a sick bay. All the gun batteries of Ouistreham and the surrounding area had links to the fire command post, something that underlines its importance.

The first British tentative to capture it on D-Day was met with a hail of grenades and heavy machine-gun fire and they did not make any further attempts, preferring to concentrate on other, higher priority objectives, and forgetting for a while this impressive angular raw concrete mass that now looked over a field of ruins.

Above: the Grand Bunker is one of the rare structures that was spared by the fighting of 6 June. In the foreground are the remains of the German defences. (Coll. © Grand Bunker.)

At the entrance to the Grand Bunker, now a museum, one can see this reconstitution of the destruction of the doors using an explosive charge.

At the entrance to the Grand Bunker, now a museum, one can see this reconstitution of the destruction of the doors using an explosive charge.

However, once quiet returned to the beaches, The British Royal Engineers headquarters decided to list all of the equipment that had been abandoned by the Germans. Thus, it was this way that, on 9 June, Lieutenant Bob Orrell of 91 Field Company, Royal Engineers, received the order to check the contents of the bunker that had been spared by the fighting of 6 June.

At around 22.00 hrs, Bob Orrell, an engineer in civilian life, arrived by vehicle at the bunker, accompanied by three men. Seeing that the entrance was blocked by two enormous armoured doors, the British sappers decided to place three kilograms of explosives on the hinges of one of the doors. The explosion caused more noise than damage and a fresh

Below: the first floor was underground and notably comprised of a room where air pumps and filters were installed.

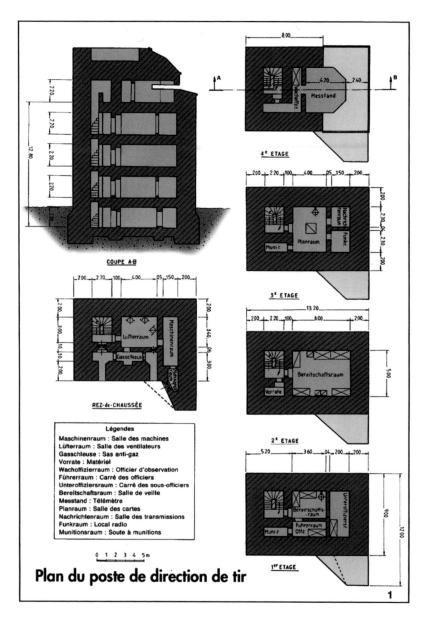

COUPE A-B

REZ-de-CHAUSSÉE

4ᵉ ETAGE

3ᵉ ETAGE

2ᵉ ETAGE

1ᵉʳ ETAGE

Légendes
Maschinenraum : Salle des machines
Lüfterraum : Salle des ventilateurs
Gasschleuse : Sas anti-gaz
Vorrate : Matériel
Wachoffizierraum : Officier d'observation
Führerraum : Carré des officiers
Unteroffiziersraum : Carré des sous-officiers
Bereitschaftsraum : Salle de veille
Messtand : Télémètre
Planraum : Salle des cartes
Nachrichtenraum : Salle des transmissions
Funkraum : Local radio
Munitionsraum : Soute à munitions

0 1 2 3 4 5m

Plan du poste de direction de tir

1

Opposite: the bunker housed technical installations (engine room, ventilation), armoury, barracks (dormitories and sick bay), a command post with telephone switchboard, radio room, observation platform and range-finder post.

Below: all of the Ouistreham gun batteries and those of the surrounding area were linked via telephone and radio to the firing command post.

Below and opposite: although the bulk of the structure was finished in November 1943, the installation of the equipment was only completed a short time before the Landings. (Coll. © Grand Bunker.)

attempt had to be made with an extra charge of five kilograms.

In all, it took Lieutenant Orrell and his men four hours to at last penetrate into the bunker. Lighting the way with their paraffin lamp, they came across crates of grenades and various items of equipment on the ground floor. But not a living soul...

Suddenly, to their great surprise, a man's voice speaking in perfect English, asked the visitors to show themselves. With caution, and who would not in such circumstances, Bob Orell answered that he preferred to see the man he was speaking with come down rather than the other way round.

The surprise felt by the British increased as they watched 53 German soldiers, two of whom were officers, come down the stairs and surrender without the slightest hint of difficulty and visibly unshaken by the last few days spent confined in the bunker. It is said that before surrendering, the small garrison had polished off all the food and drink supplies...

What is sure is that after such an easy surrender, the town of Ouistreham was now really liberated. As for the fire command post, captured in intact by the Allies, it now houses a museum called the "Grand Bunker".

The top floor houses the range-finder room, offering an uninterrupted view of the coast.

Standing seventeen metres tall, the fire command post allowed for the observation of the Bay of the Seine river across a fifty-kilometre arc. (Coll. © Grand Bunker.)

23. A big storm destroys one of the artificial harbours

On 19 June, an unusually strong storm for the time of year hit the Landings zone, causing irreversible damage to the artificial harbour of *Mulberry A*, positioned off Omaha Beach.

The engineers and logistics experts of Operation Overlord may have surpassed themselves in terms of audacity and imagination in bringing to life Lord Mountbatten's fabulous idea, but nature remained the strongest. On 19 June 1944, two weeks after D-Day, a large north-east storm blew over the Channel. It would hit hard the two artificial harbours, "Mulberry A" (A for American) off Saint-Laurent-sur-Mer (Omaha sector) and "Mulberry B" (B for British) off Arromanches and Asnelles (Gold sector), the pre-made sections of which had been brought across by sea a few days after the Landings.

A combination of high tides and wind, gusting at speeds of up to Force 8, led to the sea crashing over the breakwaters. The "Phoenix" caissons were hit particularly hard. As the latter were without decking, they filled with water and some even split due to the pressure. Of the two artificial harbours, it was, by far and away, "Mulberry A" that suffered the most serious damage. Having broken away, some parts hit others, causing fatal damage. The "Lobnitz" pier head units were damaged or totally destroyed., their floating pontoons broken up.

Due to a combination of high tides and wind that blew up to Force 8, the sea broke over the breakwaters and caused serious damage to the units of the artificial harbour.

Arromanches seen the day after the storm. Units of the artificial harbour have been driven in shore.

Having suffered much less damage, the Arromanches artificial harbour was soon put back into service.

Thanks to this photo of the artificial harbour at Arromanches, we can understand the vital role played by these breakwaters. Inside the harbour, the swell has disappeared.

On the evening of 21 June, with the wind weakening at last, the toll was terrible. Too seriously damaged, "Mulberry A" was deemed beyond repair and would have to be abandoned. As for "Mulberry B", it had been more sheltered off Arromanches, thus suffering less damage and was able to be rapidly put back into service, despite its heavy damage.

Lacking the time to rebuild the harbour, the Americans found themselves faced with a dilemma in order to carry on with the daily disembarkation of thousands of men and tonnes of supplies. They would overcome this setback by falling back on a solution that was as easy as it was efficient: by scuttling their transport ships off the beaches.

"Mulberry B" would be used up to 19 November 1944. The two artificial ports combined allowed for the unloading of two and a half million men, five-hundred thousand vehicles of all types and four million tonnes of equipment.

Although the last remains of "Mulberry A" were removed from the sea after the war, one can still see parts of "Mulberry B" off Arromanches and Asnelles, some of which are surprisingly well-preserved such a long time after D-Day.

Remains of "Mulberry B" off the cliffs of Arromanches. (Photo: Francis Cormon.)

An aerial photo of "Mulberry B" off the beaches of Arromanches and Asnelles. (Photo: Francis Cormon.)

24. Fighter planes carrying the mail

The Allies used Spitfires and Hurricanes to carry the mail, but also other items that were just as important for maintaining the morale of the troops.

A Hurricane unloading mail bags at the Bazenville/B2 airfield.

V-Mail envelope designed by the US Army's postal services.

FROM:

SEE INSTRUCTION NO. 5

V···— MAIL

TO:

V-Mail service provides a most rapid means of communication. If addressed to a place where photographing service is not available the original letter will be dispatched by the most expeditious means.

INSTRUCTIONS

(1) Write the entire message plainly on the other side within marginal lines.

(2) Print the name and address in the two spaces provided. Addresses of members of the Armed Forces should show full name, complete military or naval address, including grade or rank, serial number, unit to which assigned or attached and army post office in care of the appropriate postmaster or appropriate fleet post office.

(3) Fold, seal, and deposit in any post office letter drop or street letter box.

(4) Enclosures must not be placed in this envelope.

(5) V-Mail letters may be sent free of postage by members of the Armed Forces. When sent by others postage must be prepaid at domestic rates (3c ordinary mail, 6c if domestic air mail service is desired when mailed in the U. S.)

★ GPO 16—08168-5

FOLD TOP AND BOTTOM IN, THEN FOLD IN CENTER AND SEAL

There is nothing more important for a soldier at war, far from home, than receiving mail. As well as the comfort and pleasure derived from receiving news from loved ones, it also signified to the men that the high command had total control of lines of communications. As we can see, for the Allied Expeditionary Force, the Army Post Office would play a role that was just as vital as the medical or supply units.

The first planes to land on French soil, outside of crash landings, were the special Hawker Hurricanes of the RAF's 46th Group, tasked with transporting mail. These planes, survivors of the Battle of Britain, were stripped of their guns in order to make them lighter and faster, and they landed at Sainte-Croix-sur-Mer (between Arromanches and Courseulles-sur-Mer), at 06.30 hrs on Saturday 10 June.

Told in this way, the event might appear ordinary. It was, however, a real exploit. Indeed, only four days after the Landings, the engineers had managed to set up an airfield and make it operational. The Hurricanes brought over British mail, but also carried American messages, named V-Mail. The latter were written on special envelopes. After passing by censorship, they were put onto microfilm then sent to France from the United States. Upon arrival the negatives were blown up by an automated machine, then at last sent to their recipients. One case of microfilms replaced thirty-seven mail bags, proving the ingenuity of this system.

The problem was more straightforward for the British as they were closer to home. Thus, they retained a more traditional system, but one which was better suited to the circumstances by RAF Transport Command, who had especially created a squadron equipped with Hurricane MK II C. The airfield in France, after Sainte-Croix-sur-Mer, was Bazenville/B2. The mail was carried either in extra tanks fitted beneath the wings, or inside the plane itself.

As an aside, and the great lines of history are made up of such asides, these tanks were not only used to carry mail. On occasion they were filled with beer. It should be said that in the summer of 1944, Normandy was somewhat lacking in pubs. From an allied point of view, naturally...

A Spitfire being loaded with beer at an airfield in Great Britain.

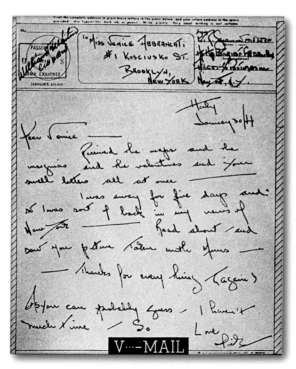

A letter that was sent by V-Mail.

77

25. PLUTO carried the black gold beneath the sea

Revolutionary for its time, the PLUTO underwater pipeline would make a vital contribution to the allied victory. It would also modernise the post-war oil industry.

The Operation Overlord planners had foreseen that by D+90 forty-five divisions would have landed, a total of two million men and 500,000 vehicles requiring 14,000 tonnes of petrol per day. The initial scheduling for petrol and lubricants (POL: Petrol-Oil-Lubricant) was carried out in three directions: the off-loading of jerricans and supply from tankers anchored off the beaches; the laying of pipelines on the bed of the Channel between England and Normandy; and finally, the use of prefabricated harbours and deep-water ports.

Supply from tankers anchored off the beaches was part of the Minor System. These ships were linked to the shore via a short pipeline (Tombola), the end of which came out of the sea and was kept afloat by buoys. Pumping stations on land carried the black gold to tanks installed near the coast.

The second phase of this petrol supply line, and the most spectacular, was the putting into service of the particularly ground-breaking PLUTO system (Pipeline Underwater Transport of Oil or Pipe Line Under The Ocean). The design of a specially adapted pipeline fell to Clifford Hartley, the chief engineer of the Anglo Iranian Oil Company (which would become British Petroleum). He worked around an underwater telephone cable, removing the copper in the middle whilst retaining the four lead and steel outer sleeves, resulting in a very heavy hollow tube. For reasons of secrecy, this pipeline was named HAIS (for Hartley Anglo Iranian Siemens).

As well as this pipeline, another was designed, with the same inner diameter, but more rigid. This was named HAMEL (the contraction of the names of its two designers: H. A. Hammick and B.J. Ellis). In order to place this pipeline on the seabed, the two engineers came up with the idea of using a giant drum towed by tugs. Conundrum (the contraction of Cone-ended-drum) was thirty metres long and twelve metres in diameter. Each drum had to be able to take 80 miles (128 km) of HAMEL cable, making a load of 1,600 tonnes.

All of the PLUTO planning rested in the capture of Cherbourg, planned for 23 June. However, the town did not fall into allied hands until the 30th and it would not be until 25 July that the first allied tanker could berth along the Querqueville sea wall.

Following the arrival of the cable ships mid-August and the putting into service of the pumping stations at Nacqueville, the first flexible HAIS cable could be put into service. At the same time, HMS Conundrum I was due to leave Southampton for Cherbourg on 25 August. Alas, it was spotted that the drum loaded with HAMEL cable, which had remained almost six months in the British port, was covered with barnacles, rendering it unusable. It

The people seen on the right give an idea of the scale of a Conundrum, a huge floating drum specially designed to lay the HAMEL pipeline across the Channel.

was only on 29 September that HMS Conundrum II, towed by three tugs, was able to lay the first HAMEL pipeline.

The pipeline from the Isle of Wight to Cherbourg, known as "Bambi", was initially supposed to comprise of four pipelines. In fact, it only had two and would be closed down on 4 October, meaning that it was only used for twelve days! With a total of 3,500 tonnes, this was a long way off what the planners had forecast... For the transportation of some of the missing tonnage, Eisenhower's logistical experts could luckily rely on the ports of Cherbourg, Saint-Vaast, Carentan, Isigny, Grandcamp, Port-en-Bessin, Arromanches, Courseulles and Ouistreham, as well as the beaches and the *Tombola* pipeline networks of the *Minor System*.

By taking into account all of the means of transportation, the allied armies received, starting from D-Day, a total of 173 million gallons of petrol, some 5.2 million tonnes. 4.3 million tonnes were unloaded from American tankers at various ports and 826,000 tonnes came directly from American refineries. PLUTO allowed for the transportation of 379,000 tonnes via 1,100 km of pipelines, making 8% of the total tonnage. And although the "Bambi Route" between the Isle of Wight and Cherbourg was only a partial success, PLUTO remains a huge technological success of which the world still reaps the benefits of its ambitious innovations.

Below: part of a land pipeline used by the Allies to transport oil.

Above: British sailors deploy the PLUTO pipeline from HMS Sancroft.

Opposite: part of a flexible HAIS pipeline showing the various sleeves: lead tube, tarred fabric, cotton sleeve, steel and copper sleeve, galvanised steel strands, plus two layers of tarred canvas in a reversed coil.

26. Mont Cauvin saved the Landings

It is not the highest hill in Normandy by a long stretch. Nevertheless, it could be said that it played an important role in the success of Operation Overlord. Belonging to the locality of Etréham, Mont Cauvin is situated a few kilometres inland, between Port-en-Bessin and Omaha Beach. If it is now known to history it is because of a delay.

Initially, the port of Cherbourg was planned to ensure the supplies of petrol to the Allies starting in early June. However, the port was not captured until 30 June. Repairing the damaged port infrastructure took such a long time that it was only on 25 July that the first tanker could berth at the Querqueville breakwater.

In the meantime, a replacement solution had to be found as troops and vehicles continued to land daily on the beaches. Thus, Mont Cauvin was hastily equipped with large tanks in order to store the precious "black gold" brought in from tankers anchored at the offshore port of Sainte-Honorine-des-Pertes. It was only gravity that carried it to the stations of Port-en-Bessin, Omaha Beach, Balleroy; not forgetting Saint-Lô, the departure point of the famous "Red Ball Express" (see chapter 31).

With Sainte-Honorine-des-Pertes and Port-en-Bessin, Mont Cauvin was the first link in the pipeline and road transportation of petrol known as the *Minor System*.

In light of the fact that a modern army cannot exist without petrol, one can say that, with its altitude of 68 metres, Mont Cauvin did, in a way, save the Landings.

Along with Sainte-Honorine-des-Pertes and Port-en-Bessin, Mont Cauvin was the first link in the pipeline and road transportation petrol network, known as the Minor System.

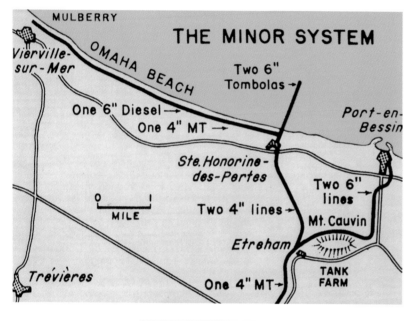

Using only gravity, the tanks at Mont Cauvin flowed to the stations at Port-en-Bessin, Omaha Beach, Balleroy and Saint-Lô.

27. Churchill flies over the beaches in a German plane

wo weeks after D-Day, Winston Churchill took off from the allied airfield coded B3, situated half way between the localities of Sainte-Croix-sur-Mer, Crépon and Ver-sur-Mer, for a flight over the landing beaches. There is nothing surprising up to this point, except for the fact that the plane in which the British Prime Minister was flying had neither been built in Great Britain, nor America. It was a Fieseler Storch 156, a German reconnaissance plane that had been captured in North Africa and used by Air Vice Marshal Harry Broadhurst. Churchill, who was also First Lord of the Admiralty, much preferred a boat to a plane. However, he allowed himself to be talked into it when he was told that the Fieseler Storch had the reputation of being able to land in a very narrow space.

A few days earlier, the same airfield had welcomed another illustrious person. At 09.35 hrs on 15 June, the B3 airfield saw the arrival of the large Boeing B-17 *"Boops"*, the personal plane of General Spaatz, carrying General Dwight Eisenhower, the Supreme Commander of the allied forces in Europe.

Present in the cockpit was Eisenhower's son, John, a US Air Force cadet, who did not hide his surprise at seeing the *"Flying Fortress"*

land *"in a field"*. Indeed, this was a veritable exploit to land such a plane on a grass airstrip that was only 1,200 metres long, when generally twice that length was required.

General Spaatz seen here in front of his B-17 "Boops" which flew General Eisenhower to Normandy on 15 June 1944.

Winston Churchill at the B3 airstrip in Normandy, on board Harry Broadhurst's (on the right) Fieseler Storch 156.

28. Ten million jerricans vanished into thin air

Out of the twenty million jerricans landed in Normandy from D-Day onwards, almost half could not be found by the end of August. This was a real conundrum for the Allies.

Copied from the *Wehrmacht Kanister* invented by the Germans in the nineteen-thirties, the jerrican replaced the old British four-gallon square petrol tin made from tin sheet metal, notably used in North Africa, but too fragile and disposable. The new petrol tin could hold four gallons (one gallon equals 4.546 litres) for the British and five gallons (one gallon equals 3.785 litres) for the Americans. This difference in quantity measurements caused a few problems for the Operation Overlord planners.

Added to this was another problem, the ramifications of which had been totally unforeseen by the Allies. Out of the twenty million that had been landed in Normandy, there were more than ten million missing at the end of August. What had happened to them? Several theories can be put forward: left behind by the tank crews and those of other vehicles, they had been used to make shelters, used as blocks in repair workshops, sold or stolen...

When we know that an American armored division used on average 90,000 litres of petrol per day when on the move, we can understand why the high command took this issue so seriously. They even went as far as setting up a large-scale recovery program. Added to the prisoners of war tasked with recovering the precious metal cans were school children. For their contribution to this unusual war effort, the French children were even rewarded with certificates signed by Eisenhower himself.

A nurse helps unload jerricans from a medical C-47 which will fly back with wounded men.

Above: General Eisenhower at Cherbourg watches as jerricans are filled using petrol captured from the Germans.

QUARTIER GÉNÉRAL SUPRÊME
FORCES EXPÉDITIONNAIRES ALLIÉES

Certificat de Mérite

L'Elève *Decaumont Pierre* a bien mérité des Armées Alliées en participant à la campagne pour la récupération des bidons d'essence dits "Jerricans".

Décerné le *19 Septembre 1944*
à l'Ecole de *Garçons d'Isigny*
Directeur

COMMANDANT SUPRÊME DES
FORCES EXPÉDITIONNAIRES ALLIÉES

A certificate awarded to French school children who brought in empty jerricans. It is signed by Eisenhower.

29. The red gold, the other "fuel" to allied success

Just as important as the transportation of oil, the packaging and transportation of blood to the battle fields played a vital role, but one which is less known, in the allied victory in Normandy.

Although the first experiments concerning blood transfusion date back to 1914, it was the Spanish Civil War, twenty years later, that really brought this technique into the modern era. Two doctors, the Canadian Norman Bethune and the British Reginald Saxton, set up a blood bank for the Republicans and put into place mobile transfusion units in which bottles of refrigerated blood were kept for almost twenty days.

Making the most of the experience gained in Spain, in 1938 and just after the Munich Crisis, the British created a central military transfusion service, equipped with a blood bank that could supply all of the transfusion units, wherever they were in the world. This was the Army Blood Transfusion Service (ABTS), stationed in Bristol during the summer of 1939, just before the general mobilisation of 3 September. Each of these Base Transfusion Units (BTU) was supplied with all of the transfusion

Previous page: wounded men being boarded before their return to England by sea.

A fleet of Norseman UC 64 A bringing blood over from England to an airfield near the sea that can be seen in the background. This photo was probably taken at Saint-Pierre-du-Mont.

YOUR BLOOD
CAN SAVE HIM

products: blood, liquid plasma liquid, powdered plasma, crystalloid fluids, serum and transfusion equipment.

This ground-breaking system, in terms of production, packaging and transport, was put to the test in the spring of 1940 in France. One of the primary tasks of the Army Blood Transfusion Service was, of course, the organisation and collecting of blood. For this, the call for donors was essential and all means of available communication were used. Thus, Great Britain was plastered with posters rivalling in persuasion, to which were added adverts in magazines and newspapers.

The constant increase in the number of donors testifies to the great mobilisation of the British people.: from 5,000 in September 1939 to 367,000 at the end of 1943; and this number would rise to almost 580,000 in May 1945. Only O group blood was kept as it was, the other groups being used to produce the various accompanying products.

On the other side of the Atlantic, the Americans lent their support to this effort. As early as June 1940, the Blood Transfusion Association (BTA) launched its "*Blood for Britain*" program, which consisted of sending plasma to Great Britain. The man in charge of this program was no other than Dr Charles R. Drew, an African

American posters for the collecting of blood and paper. The latter was used for the manufacture of plasma boxes.

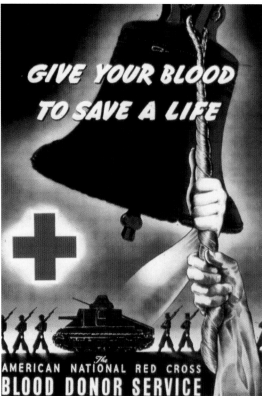

GIVE YOUR BLOOD TO SAVE A LIFE

The
AMERICAN NATIONAL RED CROSS
BLOOD DONOR SERVICE

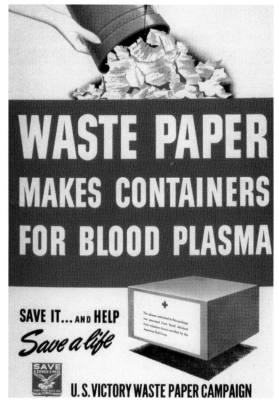

WASTE PAPER MAKES CONTAINERS FOR BLOOD PLASMA

SAVE IT... AND HELP *Save a life*

U.S. VICTORY WASTE PAPER CAMPAIGN

American doctor from Columbia University, considered as being the pioneer of blood transfusion in the USA, notably for having advised the use of the easier to use plasma along with pure blood. Indeed, plasma solved at the same time the problems of compatibility as it was no longer an obligation to take into account the blood groups of the donors and recipients. This therefore allowed fluid transfusions to be carried out whilst waiting to receive real blood.

It was no surprise, therefore, that in February 1941, Charles R. Drew was named as the first head of the American Red Cross blood bank. In November of the same year, he resigned stating that the War Department had ordered him to no longer mix the blood of blacks with that of whites. In this segregationist America, it was said that black blood was more conducive to developing venereal disease than that of whites. Whereas Dr Drew pointed out that only blood groups and Rh blood groups differentiated human blood.

The fact remains that when the United States found themselves at war following the Japanese attack on Pearl Harbor, they were far behind Great Britain in terms of blood transfusion. However, as it usually did, the richest country in the world got to grips with the problem and

The blood is taken from the refrigerator in order to be placed in thermos transportation containers to be sent to Normandy. This photo was taken on 12 June 1944.

The inside of this container holds a metal bottle with powdered blood plasma and a metal bottle containing sterilised water.

A transfusion being carried out on Utah Beach by American medics. The rifle stuck in the sand is being used to hold the plasma bottle.

soon caught up. Unlike Great Britain where there was only one blood bank and where the donors were unpaid volunteers, the USA had several operators and the donors were, either unpaid volunteers, or paid professionals.

1941 also saw the American Red Cross become the main operator and supplier to the armed forces. As was the case on the other side of the Atlantic, large-scale advertising campaigns were launched in order to attract volunteer donors. The first Red Cross Blood Donors Center (BDC) opened on 4 February 1941 and the 35th and last in 10 January 1944. From the 29,000 pints of blood collected following Pearl Harbor, this number would increase to 123,000 during the week following D-Day.

Indeed, the Landings would, by their unheard of scale and needs, speed up the modernisation and development of blood transfusions. Late 1943, early 1944, the Americans set up their first Blood Bank (BB) in Great Britain in view of D-Day. This took the form of a 250-bed general hospital in Salisbury in southern England, where only O group blood was collected. The

forecasts considered that 1,000 pints of blood would have to be supplied between D-Day and D+5.

Given the short lifespan of refrigerated blood (fourteen days), it is easy to see why air transportation was the obvious choice in taking the precious blood collected in the United States. It was for this same reason that this means of transport was chosen between England and the Continent as soon as temporary airstrips in Normandy were operational.

The C54 Skymaster plane was used to ensure the link between the USA and Great Britain. Derived from the civilian Douglas DC4 aircraft, it could fly at a speed of 400 kph and had a range of 6,400 km. In the days following the Landings, it would also be used for to take back wounded men. As well as being used to drop paratroopers, the DC3/C47 Skytrain, better known under the name of Dakota, was used to transport blood between England and Normandy. Finally, it was the small single-engine Canadian UC 64 Norseman, a plane capable of landing everywhere, that was used to take the blood containers up to the frontline.

With the sun still not risen on Tuesday 6 June 1944, the crash of a 101st Airborne glider in the landing zone wounded 25 men. They were all given transfusions using plasma carried by the medical units. A few hours later, the first American hospital was set up at the *château de Colombières*, near Sainte-Marie-du-Mont.

On D+1, the first refrigerated truck landed on Normandy soil with its 80 pints of blood. On D+10, Lieutenant Reardon's Blood Bank buried in the ground his large Navy-type refrigerator in which he stored 300 pints of blood. Reardon was equipped with eight refrigerated trucks each containing 80 pints of blood for the surgical units of the 1st US Army. At the beginning of August, the arrival of the 3rd US Army required an increase of 150 pints per day, which soon grew to an extra 500 pints.

In June 1944, this ratio, which improved throughout time, could change according to the various US armies engaged on the European front. For all of these armies, the average ratio was one pint for 1.33 wounded throughout the entire length of the European campaign.

During the night of 5-6 June in the British sector, the parachutists and gliders landed around the bridges at Ranville and Bénouville. These first men in action had almost 200 plasma bottles at their disposal, making approximately two per man. Losses were heavy and many transfusions had to be carried out where the men lay. The following days saw the landing and installation of the thirteen Field Transmission Units as close as possible to the fighting units, forming the framework of transfusion organisation of the British Liberation Army. These mobile FTU set up notably at Asnelles, Ver, Graye, Bernières, Bretteville-l'Orgueille-use, Cheux, Hermanville, Secqueville-en-Bessin, Putot-en-Bessin, Loucelles and Mouen.

The central blood bank was set up at Bayeux. As soon as the temporary airstrips were operational, aircraft became the preferred means of supply transport. It was from there that, throughout the summer, blood and plasma bottles destined for twenty field hospitals were transported, for a total of some 20,000 beds.

For all of the 21st Army Group units, there were 144,649 wounded between 6 June 1944 to 8 May 1945, 12% of which received one or several transfusions. 75% of the wounded survived, the others died in forward aid posts.

The allied mobilisation for blood continued uninterrupted. Throughout the European campaign, from August 1944 to May 1945, the United States sent over 201,105 pints of blood. And from April 44 to May 45, the US Army would produce, in Great Britain, 103,649 pints of American blood, 14,475 pints of British blood and 12,466 pints of "European" blood (French, Belgian and German prisoner of war donors).

At the end of the war, the Americans had received 13 million blood donations, a figure that should be compared to their 488,550 wounded treated in Europe.

General Montgomery, commander of the allied 21st Army Group, visits the blood bank at Bayeux in the summer of 1944.

89

30. "Blood shells" for the GIs surrounded at Mortain

At Mortain, the American artillerymen played at being chemists in order to supply the infantrymen, surrounded by Germans, with medicine and blood plasma. This exploit is as unusual as it is little known in the story of the Battle of Normandy.

In early August 1944, the troops of General Patton were thrusting towards Brittany and Le Mans. During the night of 6-7 August, the Germans launched a counter-attack against the right flank of the allied forces in the region of Mortain. This was Operation *Lüttich* (Liege in German), ordered by Hitler himself in order to split the 1st and 3rd US Armies. On Hill 317, to the east of Mortain, the 2nd Battalion of the 30th Infantry Division came under intense artillery fire, beginning in the morning and which cut it off from the rest of the division. They held a strategic position which overlooked the entire Cance valley and the town.

At the price of heavy casualties, for six days the GIs withstood the attacks led by the *SS* soldiers of the 2nd panzer division. Completely cut-off, they were unable to receive any supplies. Their situation became so alarming that an attempt was made to drop medical supplies by parachute, but the containers fell into the enemy lines.

It was at this point that the Psychological Warfare specialists, based south of Cherbourg, came up with the idea of firing shells to the encircled troops in which leaflets were replaced with penicillin, sulphonamide, plasma (powdered plasma and sterilised water to mix the plasma) and morphine. The ammunition chosen for this special type of "bombardment" were 105 and 155 mm shells used for, as well as firing leaflets, creating smoke.

Preparing the load of a smoke shell. Note in this photo the use of chocolate bars acting as thermal and mechanical buffers between the medicine bottles.

Above: the cover of Time, dated 21 August 1944, in which the story is told of the first use of "blood shells" during the Mortain counter-attack.

For this new type of usage, the medicine was solidly held down inside the shells and any empty space was filled with...chocolate bars.

Despite all off the efforts of the artillerymen in their role as chemists, this last chance operation was met with mixed success. On the morning of 12 August, the surrounded soldiers were at last relieved, thanks to the arrival of reinforcements from the 35th Infantry Division. Out of the 950 men that the unit, now known as "The lost battalion" had at the beginning, only 375 were still fit to fight.

This little-known episode of the Battle of Normandy was deemed to be so extraordinary that it was told by Captain R.D. Keyley in a Time article dated 21 August and called *"A Hell of a Nerve"*.

As for the "blood shells", they were upgraded following their baptism of fire at Mortain and were used again, a few months later, during the Battle of the Bulge.

Filling a 155 HC smoke shell with medicine destined for the surrounded troops.

Setting the fuse that will free the load consisting of medicine supplies.

32. When the water of Normandy gave the Allies air superiority

As was the case with petrol and blood for transfusions, water was the subject of special logistical management during Operation Overlord.

The allied planners forecast a requirement of one gallon (4.5 litres) per man per day, plus ten gallons for a hospital bed. In the early days of the Landings, as much water was brought ashore as petrol, in tankers or jerricans.

Once landed, the troops would use local wells as soon as the water was quality controlled. Thus, the well of Mare Saint Pierre, in Hermanville, was mentioned in British Army dispatches for having provided 1.5 million gallons of water from 6 June to 1 July!

Added to this was water from rivers such as the Aure, Seulles, Thue and Mue, which was treated and distributed. Finally, in order to deal with rising demand, twenty-eight wells were bored, some of which remain in use to this day, like at Banville.

As well as water for personal use and in hospitals, it was also needed for the washing of clothing. This led to the setting up of a large industrial laundry at Pierrepont on the river Thue. The Allies also needed water to clean their vehicles and for firefighting. In short, throughout the summer of 1944, the men of the Royal Engineers tasked with the "Water Scheme" were kept busy.

This was even more so given the fact that they had to deal with another challenge, the extent of which they had not foreseen. Indeed, it soon became obvious that the dozens of earth runways made for allied planes created clouds of dust. This meant that some engines, the air intakes of which were not suited for these "African" conditions, had a length of use of only forty-eight hours! Initially, whilst awaiting something better, fuel was sprayed onto the airstrips at the risk of rendering them slippery.

The British engineers would have to, therefore, create a second water network alongside that of drinking water, in order to spray the airstrips at night and reduce the dust. The same rivers were used and around ten pump houses, in various locations, with pipeline networks, were built in record time. There are a few of these pump houses still in existence, notably at Vaux-sur-Seulles and Saint-Gabriel-Brécy.

Built by the British Royal Engineers in 1944 at Saint-Gabriel-Brécy, this pump house took water from the river Seulles to supply in priority the nearby allied airfields. It was purchased in 1974 by one of the authors of this book.

Above: this inscription on one of the side-walls of the pump house at Saint-Gabriel-Brécy shows the year of its construction.

Opposite: the same wall bears this Greek inscription which signifies "water is best" (to be understood in the sense of goodness). This is the first verse of the Ode to nature by the Ancient Greek poet, Pindar. The same inscription can be seen on the lintel of the Roman Baths Pump Room in the town of Bath, south-west England.

33. A discovery between Caen and Falaise which sends shivers down the spine

In August 1944, the Canadians discovered in the Calvados a full-size mock-up of a V-2 rocket. The Germans had set up numerous firing platforms for the V-1 and V-2 in Normandy.

Its proximity to the English coast meant that Normandy, and northern France, were ideal sites for the new V-weapons (V for *Vergeltung*, Vengeance) that had been developed by the *Third Reich*. Although there are more than two-hundred V-1 launch sites known in France, those for the V-2 are more difficult to list. Indeed, following the huge concrete construction sites, in the summer of 1944 the sites were more often 20 by 10 metre launch pads, set up in various areas and which were much less visible.

We should remember that the V-1 was a small pilot-less plane, made by Fieseler and equipped with a pulsejet engine. Eight metres in length and with a 5.40 metre wingspan, it was able to carry a 850 kg explosive payload over a distance of up to 300 kilometres at a speed of 650 kph. 35,000 were built by Volkswagen. Barrage balloon cables and above all British fighter planes cut down the number of V-1 impacts. Whilst on this subject, we should note that one of the RAF aces, the Le Havre born Jean Maridor, ended up losing his life whilst shooting down his sixth V-1 on 3 August 1944.

The V-2 was an intercontinental missile with a liquid-propellant engine, 14 metres in length and capable of carrying a one-tonne payload over 350 kilometres at a speed of 5,000 kph, flying at an altitude of 85 kilometres. 10,000 of these rockets were made. This missile, the forebear of the first rockets used in the conquest of space, was undetectable by radar at the time and invulnerable to any means of interception.

At the time of the Battle of Normandy, eighteen V-1 launch sites undergoing construction were listed in the Calvados, fourteen in the Manche and eleven in the Seine-Maritime. In the latter department, there were also eleven operational V-1 launch sites. Amongst these

sites was that of Val Ygot, at Ardouval, which can be visited today and shows in detail a complete launch site.

Although the Allies very quickly found out what the V-1 was, the same could not be said for the V-2. Of course there were aerial photos from Peenemünde (the manufacture and test site for the missiles) in the Baltic Sea, which

The Aucrais quarries where, in August 1944, the Canadians found a life-size V-2 mock-up, used to test movement in the tunnels.

A V-2 on its
launch pad.

Below: an aerial photograph taken by the Allies at the
Peenemünde manufacture and test site on the Baltic Sea.

Below: american soldiers look at V-1 flying bombs
at the exit of an underground factory in Germany. The V-1 was made by deported prisoners.

revealed machines even more impressive than
the V-1, but they had been unable to accurately
identify the type.

It was not until the month of August 1944 that
identification was possible, with the Canadian
discovery of a life-size mock-up of a V-2 in
the Aucrais quarries, used to test movement
in the tunnels. The command post was based
at Isigny-sur-Mer and a few launch pads had
been set up nearby, notably at Le Molay-Littry.
The liquid oxygen factory was at Pont-d'Ouil-
ly and the assembly plant at Sottevast. All of
the various sites were linked by rail.

34. De Gaulle did not want the American "fake money"

Thanks to François Coulet, the very first French Republic commissioner, De Gaulle was able to impose the authority of his provisional government. This meant that France was able to avoid bank notes printed by the Americans.

De Gaulle landed on the beach of Cour-seulles-sur-Mer on 14 June 1944. The name of the destroyer that brought him over from England, *La Com-battante*, sums up the four long years that it had taken to impose Free France. Impose, well not entirely... Indeed, the Americans remained unconvinced and they had planned to place France under AMGOT control (Allied Military Government of Occupied Territories), tasked with administration of liberated areas until the establishment of a legitimate government, that is to say elected by the people. De Gaulle did not want anything to do with AMGOT, so dear to Roosevelt, and did not hesitate in calling these new bank notes *"fake money"*.

In order to put across his point of view, De Gaulle could rely on François Coulet who had been named two days earlier as *"Republican commissioner for liberated areas"*. He knew this 38-year old Montpellier-born diplomat well, and placed total trust in him. Based in Helsinki when war was declared, François Coulet had joined the Free French as early as June 1940, becoming General De Gaulle's chief of staff in 1941, then commander of parachute infantry.

In September 1943, De Gaulle sent him to Corsica as general secretary of the police force. With his diplomatic skills, François Coulet successfully managed the transition from the Vichy government to that which Free France wanted to install. With his mission

Bayeux, 14 June 1944. After an enthusiastic welcome from the population, De Gaulle gave a speech which, before passing into history, confirmed his legitimate place as head of a liberated France.

2 francs AMGOT banknote based on the American dollar. There were also 5, 10, 50 and 100 francs notes. These banknotes were hated by De Gaulle who called them *"fake money"*.

Below: 9 June 1944, François Coulet (left) In conversation with general Kœnig, leader of the FFI (centre) and General Montgomery, commander of the allied 21st Army Group.

accomplished on the *"Isle of Beauty"*, he was tasked by General De Gaulle with managing this transition in areas liberated following the Landings.

He accompanied De Gaulle to Bayeux where, on 14 June 1944 the head of Free France received an enthusiastic welcome from the population which, before entering into history, confirmed his legitimate place as head of a France not yet totally liberated.

As soon as he took up his position, François Coulet set up the authority of the provisional government by proceeding with several nominations: Raymond Triboulet as deputy prefect of Bayeux, then, with the liberation of Caen, Pierre Daure, known as Denis in the French Resistance, as the prefect of the Calvados department.

In August 1944, he was based in Rouen when he was called to a new position by De Gaulle: Republican commissioner for inter-allied liaison.

Who was informing the bishop in June 44?

A short time after taking up his position, François Coulet asked for a meeting with the bishop of Bayeux, *Monseigneur* Picaud, in order to, notably, hold a *Te Deum* Eucharist mass in the cathedral on 18 June, the anniversary date of De Gaulle's famous appeal on the BBC wavelengths on 18 June 1940.

The bishop gave a somewhat frosty welcome to the commissioner on 16 June. The meeting took a surprising turn, as recounted by François Coulet: *"Monsieur, I know you. You are a Protestant like your brother in law, Monsieur Daure, and I am very surprised that General de Gaulle should choose someone of the Augsburg Confession."*

So who, given that the bishop had no more links with Vatican, had been able to provide so many details concerning the personality and religion of the somewhat unknown new Republican commissioner, recently appointed in London?

It is very possible that it was the American secret services who wished to discredit François Coulet with the bishop of Bayeux. It goes to show that AMGOT was already being put into place only ten days after the Landings.

35. Bayeux, the first French town to have its by-pass

The British began its construction June 1944 so that tanks and truck convoys could avoid going through the town. The Bayeux By-Pass was the very first road of this type in France.

Beginning in the summer of 1944, the By-Pass allowed the Allies to go around Bayeux in order to supply the men on the front-line.

Situated less than ten kilometres from the sea and in the centre of the zone chosen for the Landings, Bayeux had everything going for it in order to be bombed, or simply erased from the map, like so many other Normandy towns. However, it escaped unscathed from shells or bombs that fell during D-Day. The British tank crews of the 4/7th Dragoon Guards (8th Armoured Brigade) which rolled into the town mid-morning on 7 June 1944 could therefore admire an intact medieval town built around its cathedral, with its magnificent mansion houses dating from the Renaissance period to the *Ancien Régime*.

However, every coin has its flip side. The narrow streets that had hardly changed over the course of centuries, and the road network that converged on the town, were nothing but a series of obstacles for an advancing mechanised army. It was impossible for tanks to go through the town and it was not ideal either for heavy trucks loaded with men and equipment. Basically, the Allies absolutely had to find a way of by-passing Bayeux in order to ensure the re-supplying of men on the front-line.

Below: British trucks on the northern part of the By-Pass near the bridge crossing the Aure and today's swimming pool. In the foreground one can see the metal trellis panels placed on the ground.

It was for this reason that the Royal Engineers built a By-Pass, clearing the way with bulldozers. As there was no time to lay a tarmac road, wide metal trellis panels reinforced with concrete rods were laid down. A first section of road allowed for the linking up of the Arromanches road with the Bayeux train station and the road to Tilly-sur-Seulles. A second section was put into service using the road from Arromanches.

When it was dry, the truck convoys threw up huge dust clouds. However, when it rained, this new road became a river of mud. But good or bad, this first French By-Pass fulfilled its role. Here and there, the British installed roundabouts, something else that had never been seen by the French. Added to these modifications, the British widened the *Nationale 13* road from one of Bayeux to the other and added another lane to the road to Tilly-sur-Seulles.

Soon, allied officers and war correspondents set up their billets in the best hotels in Bayeux; the *Lion d'Or* and the *Luxembourg*. As for the other ranks, without washing facilities, they had to make do with communal baths in the Aure, the river that flows through the town.

Upon the initiative of François Coulet, the Republican commissioner named by De Gaulle, Paul Vigourou d'Arvieu created the first newspaper of liberated France, the *La Renaissance du Bessin*, on 17 June, with the first issue, of which four thousand were printed, coming out on 23 June. Well, it was not exactly the first as under AMGOT the Allies got there first by starting the Liberator newspaper in Isigny. The latter did not last for long as its publication was halted following the liberation of Cherbourg.

As for the Bayeux By-Pass, it is still in use today, even if its name had been *"Frenchified"* by the Bayeux population to *"bipasse"*. It was built thirty years before the Parisian By-Pass that was opened on 25 April 1973.

The first issue of the *Renaissance du Bessin*, the first newspaper of a liberated France, which came out on 23 June 1944.

British soldiers in the Aure, the river that flows through the town.

36. General Montgomery sets up his headquarters at Creully

Two days after the Landings, the allied 21st Army Group set up its headquarters at Creully, between Bayeux and Caen, in the château de Creullet at the foot of the medieval castle.

Situated seven kilometres from the beaches, between Bayeux and Caen, Creully was liberated on the afternoon of D-Day. Two days later, General Montgomery, commander of the 21st Army Group, entered the locality. He placed his headquarters caravan, hidden by hay bales, in the park of the *château de Creullet*, at the foot of Creully castle.

With various commands setting up in the large farm of Creullet, the BBC deployed its aerials at the top of the medieval castle's tower from where it broadcast daily news concerning the unfolding battle. What is less well-known is that the *château* also housed "Monty's" special scientific services tasked with strategic research.

With the rumour afoot that some German officers, taken by surprise by the unexpected arrival of the Allies, were still hiding in the rafters, the General, almost always clothed with corduroy trousers and a polo-neck sweater, received illustrious visitors. On 12 June, he welcomed Winston Churchill in the great salon; the 14th, General De Gaulle came to visit before giving his historic speech at Bayeux;

Creully castle where a mess was installed, as well as the BBC aerials in June 1944.

Above: Montgomery is visited by General de Gaulle at Creullet on 14 June 1944.

The quartermaster services set up a high-quality mess in the *château de Creully* where 21st Army Group officers met Canadian pilots from the nearby airfield, and BBC war correspondents.

Creully church seen here with a British flail tank, the chains of which attached to the front were used for clearing mines. The photo was seemingly taken on 7 June 1944.

Montgomery personally welcomed King George VI to the *château de Creullet* on 16 June 1944.

on the 15th, it was General Eisenhower's turn, with King George VI going through the castle gates the following day.

The walls of Creullet must still resonate with the raised voice of Arthur Tedder, the Deputy Supreme Commander of Operation Overlord, demanding sites for his airfields for which "Monty" was delaying the freeing up of space necessary for their construction south of Caen. The walls should also remember how the French general Koenig, the hero of Bir-Hakeim, defended De Gaulle's commissioner, François Coulet, by informing him that he was a protestant like him.

In between headquarters meetings and the welcoming of prestigious guests, Montgomery relaxed in the park by playing with his two young dogs, "Hitler" and "Rommel", soothed by the singing of his canaries.

Every day in the main square of Creully, a truck equipped with loudspeakers broadcast news from the front-line and a band played dawn serenades in the bandstand. On Sundays, soldiers went to the service in the church and children cadged sweets from the numerous military personnel who passed through the locality.

At Creully castle, the quartermaster services set up a high-quality mess where Canadian pilots from the nearby airfield mixed with BBC correspondents, including the famous Franck Gillard. When peace returned, all of these people met in London at the exclusive "Creully Club" where they could chat about the good times they had in a pretty little Normandy village that had been spared from the bombardments.

37. The Bailey bridge gave the Allies seven-league boots

Considered by Eisenhower as one of the three major innovations of the Second World War, along with radar and heavy bombers, the Bailey bridge played a vital role in the advance of the allied armies from Normandy and into the heart of Germany.

Although it is less well-known to the wider public than the Jeep or the jerrican, the Bailey bridge nevertheless is high up on the list of striking technical innovations of the Second World War. At the very start of the Battle of Normandy, the Americans, and the British, put this modular structure to

The large construction site of the Vaucelles bridge in Caen. The Citroën garage is in the background.

great use, replacing damaged bridges, or those destroyed by allied planes or blown up by the Germans.

This ingenious set of equipment owes its name to its designer, Donald Bailey who was born in 1901 at Rotherham in Yorkshire. Fascinated by mechanics, he joined Sheffield University in 1919 where he studied engineering. He graduated in 1923 as a Bachelor of Civil Engineering. In 1928, after spotting a job advertisement with the British Army, Donald Bailey joined the Experimental Bridging Establishment (EBE), at Christchurch, as a civil engineer.

The young engineer soon showed the extent of his talent. In 1936, he made a working drawing of the famous bridge that would ensure his place in the annals of history. Three years later, war broke out. Although the Royal Air Force could count on the Hurricane and its latest plane, the Spitfire, the armoured units lagged behind and were inferior in all ways compared to their German counterparts.

As for the Royal Engineers, their mobile bridges mostly dated back to the Great War and would prove to be inadequate in the face of the mobile warfare carried out by the German army. Faced with this worrying situation, the British high command put out a tender to the various organisations that were competent in this field, in order to see if they could come up with a bridge design.

Due to a lack of means, the truss bridge thought up by Bailey remained hidden away until the winter of 1940. A Royal Engineers colonel, visiting Christchurch, met Donald Bailey and the latter sketched his modular bridge design, that he imagined like a Meccano construction, on the back of an old envelope. The officer was taken by the idea, no doubt because no other alternative had yet been proposed.

However, on 14 February 1941, Bailey received a letter requesting him to make a full-size example of his modular bridge for 1 May. The timescale was very short given the type of structure. But Bailey, who had become chief engineer of the EBE in this same year, deemed that this ambitious objective was achievable by his team.

Even simplified, the specifications remained restrictive. The clause stating that the bridge would have to able to be built rapidly and without heavy machinery imposed the obligation that each part could be carried by a maximum of six men. Thus, the primary element was a steel panel, 5 feet by 10 (1.5 m by 3), comprising of only seventeen parts. Its weight of 285 kg made it the heaviest component of the bridge. Also, all of the parts had to be transportable by truck, or plane (DC 3). The beam, comprising of panels assembled with connecting pins, chord bolts or bracing bolts, could be doubled or tripled in order to increase the length depending on the load it had to bear.

The first trials took place at the end of April on the river Stroud, near the Christchurch airfield. A 70-feet (21-metres) bridge was constructed at 2 p.m. on the planned date of 1 May. At 2.36 p.m., the truck that had carried the elements crossed the river without any difficulty. It had only taken Donald Bailey a little more than half an hour to give a startling demonstration of his invention's capacities.

As we have seen, the main special aspect of Bailey bridges was the great ease with which

Floats used for the construction of Bailey pontoon bridges.

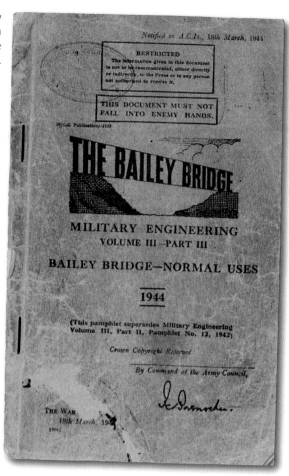

Notified in A.C.Is., 18th March, 1944

RESTRICTED

The information given in this document is not to be communicated, either directly or indirectly, to the Press or to any person not authorized to receive it.

THIS DOCUMENT MUST NOT FALL INTO ENEMY HANDS.

26/G.S. Publication/1123

THE BAILEY BRIDGE

MILITARY ENGINEERING
VOLUME III—PART III
BAILEY BRIDGE—NORMAL USES

1944

(This pamphlet supersedes Military Engineering Volume III, Part II, Pamphlet No. 12, 1942)

Crown Copyright Reserved

By Command of the Army Council,

THE WAR
18th March, 19

A 5 feet by 10 panel carried by six Royal Engineers sappers.

they could be built without the need for heavy machinery. Each ten by five foot panel, weighing 285 kg, could easily be carried by six men. A Bridging Platoon, comprising of forty sappers, could build a Class 40 (for 40 tons) bridge in two or three hours, and this was for an 80 feet (24 metres) crossing. The panels were attached by six-pound pins driven in with sledgehammers, as well as chord bolts and bracing bolts. All of these parts were standard and interchangeable.

Another advantage of the Bailey design lay in the fact that it could be adapted according to loads and span. Thus, the Class 40 bridge could be made in seven combinations: Single-Single (SS) for one truss and one storey, Triple-Single (TS) for a triple truss and one storey, Double-Double (DD) for a double truss and two storeys, Triple Double (TD) for a triple truss and two storeys, Double-Triple (DT) for a double truss and three storeys, Triple-Triple (TT) for a triple truss and three storeys.

Bailey bridges could be mounted on pillars or on specially designed pontoons. As soon as they were built, the bridges were primed with explosive charges in order to be blown up in

Building a Bailey Bridge on pontoons near Pegasus Bridge, late June 1944.

the event of a withdrawal. For night-time construction, the sappers were equipped with special hammers to dampen the noise.

Large-scale construction began in July 1941 and involved no less than six-hundred and fifty British companies. The Americans and Canadians would also make their own Bailey bridges, the parts of which were, in principal, interchangeable with those of the British.

As you might expect, it was Normandy that saw the largest use of the Bailey bridge by some two million allied soldiers and thousands of vehicles of all types that landed between 6 June and 25 August 1944. For Montgomery's British 21st Army Group alone, one thousand five-hundred Bailey bridges were used during the advance of the British, Canadian and Polish divisions, from the Battle of Normandy to the German surrender. Between Ouistreham and Caen, the Royal Engineers built twenty-one bridges over the Orne and the Caen to the sea canal.

There were almost twenty bridges over the river Dives, from Vendeuvres to Dives-sur-Mer

passing via Troarn. The first of these bridges was built over the Caen to the sea canal south of Pegasus Bridge the 17th Field Company and 263rd Field Company, Royal Engineers, British 3rd Division. Shortly afterwards, the Canadians built bridges at Reviers and Colombiers-sur-Seulles.

These first elements of the pre-fabricated bridges were landed on the beaches as early as 6 June 1944. All types of bridge and walkways later arrived via the artificial port at Arromanches that became partially operational on 12-13 June. They were then stored at the large supply British supply base at Saint Martin-des-Entrées, on the outskirts of Bayeux. One of the big advantages of this base is that it was directly linked to the Paris-Cherbourg railway.

The most serious problems that faced the allied sappers came with crossing the river Seine. This was due to the width of the river, exceeding two-hundred and fifty metres in places, and also the effect of the tides. In all, eight bridges were built over the Seine, measuring between four-hundred and fifty and seven-hundred and fifty feet.

With the crossing of the Seine and the Eure, we can estimate approximately five-hundred bridges built by the British in Normandy, from the beaches to its most easterly area. The Americans and general Leclerc's 2nd *division blindée* (French armoured division) built an equivalent number of Bailey bridges. By counting the bridges built by the British, Canadians, Poles, Americans and French, we can make an estimation of almost one thousand Bailey bridges built in Normandy.

As the Battle of Normandy came to an end, Paris celebrated its liberation with American troops and Leclerc's *2e DB* parading on the Champs-Elysées. Bradley, De Gaulle, Leclerc and Koenig watched the victory parade from a platform that was no other than... an up-side-down Bailey Bridge.

As surprising as it may seem, Donald Bailey's existence was kept secret throughout most of the war, proof of his importance in the eyes of the allied authorities. It was only on 1 July 1944 that an article in The Sphere magazine allowed the British people to put a face to this name. The French were able to make the same discovery when reading the propaganda newspaper, *Voir*, which was dropped by the Royal Air Force during the nights of 15 to 16, and 28 to 29 July 1944.

Donald Bailey died on 4 May 1985 at the age of 84. As is often the case with great inventors, his invention has outlived him. Modular and mobile bridges are still in existence. They are all made in industrialised countries by companies who no longer make any reference to the designer. However, there is one exception. Indeed, at Fort Payne, Alabama, there is a company called Bailey Bridges Inc, which continues to make the M2 American version of the Bailey Bridge.

Construction of the *London 2* bridge upstream from the Ranville bridge over the Orne near Pegasus Bridge.

Tanks crossing the *London 2* bridge.

Above: a soldier guides a flail tank over a Bailey Bridge.

Christchurch Times, Sat. April 28, 1945

S. McMULLEY LTD
BUILDING CONTRACTORS
PUREWELL BUILDING WORKS
FOR ALL CLASSES OF
:: BUILDING WORK ::
Tel : Christchurch 996

Christchurch Times

SOUTHBOURNE, HIGHCLIFFE, HURN & NEW MILTON ADVERTISER

No. 4292 [REGISTERED AS A NEWSPAPER]   SATURDAY, APRIL 28, 1945   [FOUNDED IN 1855]   Price 1½d.

EBBORN'S
The Reliable Chemists
43 HIGH STREET
CHRISTCHURCH
PHONE 276
R. A. EBBORN M.P.S. (LOND.)

THE BAILEY BRIDGE INVENTED IN CHRISTCHURCH

Product of Experimental Bridging Establishment

WORLD-FAMED EQUIPMENT FIRST MADE HERE

IT was not without justification that a British Tommy once said that the three best-known names in the Army were Eisenhower, Montgomery and Bailey; for, from the time the fighting forces first started crossing rivers in Italy right up to the crossings of the Rhine and the Elbe in Germany, one of the most important items of equipment has been the now famous Bailey Bridge.

ON THE WAY TO VICTORY — A BAILEY BRIDGE IN FRANCE

HUNDREDS of British tanks were used in the attack launched by General Montgomery east of the River Orne and south east of Caen on July 18th, 1944. The sudden offensive created one of the biggest surprises since D-Day and paved the way for the break through of the British armour into the open country beyond Caen. The above is a picture of the Bailey Bridge by which our troops crossed the Caen Canal

PROGRESS OF MORAL WELFARE SOCIETY

Co-operation between Church and State

THE annual meeting of the New Forest Area Association for Moral Welfare was held at the Town Hall, Christchurch, on Tuesday, April 20th, the Lord Bishop of Winchester (the Right Rev. Mervyn Haigh, D.D.) in the chair. It was revealed by the various reports that were read by the society had been doing excellent work, and that the worker, Miss J. Chatterton, had rendered untiring assistance in the many cases which have come to the notice of the society.

The Lord Bishop of Winchester commented upon the increased co-operation between the Church and the State. The Hampshire County Council has approved the recommendation that there should be the closest co-operation between the moral welfare workers, the health authorities and the county diocese. There had always been happy relations between the moral welfare workers and the authorities, but these relations had now received official status and approval.

Another important matter was the decision of the County Council to open three new mother and baby homes in the county. Only one would be in the Diocese of Winchester, but they were all to be staffed by a matron and three sisters, a handsome provision compared with some scenes. The diocese was to be given an effective voice in the selection of the matron and nursery sisters. That represented a big advance.

Further development in the field of co-operation between Church and State was that the County Council were to make a grant to the Diocese this year of £140.

Then there was the new develop-

ATTEMPT TO EVADE CUSTOMS

Fine of £125 Imposed

AT Christchurch Magistrates Court on Monday, William John Glasson, 41, Bedford Street, Bletchley, was charged with being knowingly concerned in a fraudulent attempt at evasion of the duties of the Customs on three watches and five bracelets. Accused pleaded guilty.

Prosecuting for the Commissioners of Customs and Excise, Mr. P. R. C. Noble said that the defendant was an official of the Foreign Office returning home to report to his Department. He had two holdalls and an attache case, and on coming to the customs barrier was given a notice instructing him to declare all articles obtained abroad. Defendant declared three bottles of port and a quarter of a pound of tobacco. When asked if he possessed any presents he was bringing into this country, Glasson said that he had nothing more to declare. The officer, on examining the holdall, discovered an empty watch case, and when questioned defendant produced the watch which he was wearing on his left wrist. At that time accused said that he had owned the watch for two years. Later he said six months, and finally admitted that he had purchased it about a month prior to his arrival in this country. Even then, defendant made no reference to two other watches which he possessed, or to the five bracelets which were discovered packed within socks in shoes.

If accused had possessed the watch for two years, it would not have been a new watch, and would have been allowed into this country duty-free. There was, said the prosecution, a definite endeavour to evade the customs. The other watches were found at the bottom of the holdalls. De-

The front page of the 28 April 1945 edition of the *Christchurch Times*, revealing that the Bailey Bridge had been invented in Christchurch.

38. Previously unpublished photos from a "Top Secret" British report

The following photos are exceptional in that up to now, they have never been seen by the public. Most of them were taken in the Gold Beach and Juno Beach sectors on 6, 7 and 8 June 1944.

In the 1970s, the widow of a high-ranking British officer discovered, in her husband's papers, a thick, black canvas-covered 41-pages, 24 x 30 cm notebook containing a little over two hundred photographs that had been stuck to the pages with tape. Most of them had been taken on 6, 7 and 8 June 1944 on Gold Beach and Juno Beach where, at dawn on D-Day, the British 50th Division and the 3rd Canadian Infantry Division had respectively landed. Some photos were taken by planes flying over the beaches at low altitude, others from beached ships or those anchored offshore.

As well as these photographs, this "Top Secret" stamped document was filled with maps and very precise information, such as times and tidal coefficients, or even water heights for the month of June 1944. The entire notebook forms an exceptional eye-witness account, and one which is incontestable concerning the reality of the landing operations in these two sectors of Operation Neptune (the naval part of Operation Overlord).

It was at the heart of Gold Beach, at Ver-sur-Mer, in the Jacquot pharmacy, that the British Admiralty in France set up its quarters, led by Admiral Sir Bertram Ramsay, Naval

A tank stuck up to its turret in the peat at the top of La Rivière beach.

Commander-in-Chief of the Allied Naval Expeditionary Force. This may well explain the origin of this enquiry report and the particular attention that was paid to it.

Shortly after its discovery, it came into our possession, once we had promised to never reveal the names of the people we acquired it from. The study of the enclosed photographs led to two major observations:

– Some enemy fortified defences seem to have been hastily built using whatever was available; wood, earth, corrugated iron, as if the imminent invasion was expected on this coast. Given the fact that the *Organisation Todt* normally used better quality materials, we can legitimately ask the question: Did the Germans know? The careful reading of the captions accompanying the photos tends to show that their author knew the answer. Indeed, he uses three times the word *"improvised"* and once the expression *"very recent"*, and notes the presence of unusual and unexpected anti-tank guns on the Atlantic Wall.

– Seeing all these allied vehicles, tanks or trucks, immobilised on the beaches, it is obvious that the type of ground and sub-soil turned out to be very different from that expected by the planners, nonetheless so meticulous, for the Landings. Indeed, neither the description of the peat bogs by the Romans, nor the brochures and postcards of the 1930s, or the work undertaken by geographers and geologists from the universities of Cambridge and Oxford, or Caen, the thousands of aerial photographs, as well as the samples and topographical surveys brought back by the intrepid frogmen, had allowed them to determine with sufficient accuracy the such richly varied soils of the Calvados coastline.

The La Rivière beach. The view of the top of a tank shows the nature of the peat.

Below: a DD (Duplex-Drive) tank stuck in the peat on the beach of Ver-sur-Mer.

German prisoners
on the beach of
Ver-sur-Mer.

Trying to pull
out a truck.

Below: a Duplex-Drive
tank abandoned in
front of a seawall
at Bernières.

Left: an allied soldier looks at a German anti-tank gun hidden in an improvised fortification in the dunes between Bernières and Courseulles.

Opposite: the same fortification seen from a different angle.

Ver-sur-Mer. A machine-gun nest reveals a very recently made position using planks taken from houses.

German obstacles known as "Belgian Gates" on the beach of Courseulles.

Above: Courseulles. An anti-tank ditch with anti-infantry wire.

Above, right: a gun and crane bogged down on the beach of Ver-sur-Mer.

Opposite: Courseulles. The front of a casemate showing the gun embrasure filled, in an improvised fashion, with earth.

LCVP leaving the beach at Grayes-sur-Mer to the west of Courseulles.

LCT approaching the Gooseberry artificial breakwater off the coast of Courseulles.

Cargo ship off Courseulles.

LCVP landing craft off Ver-sur-Mer.

The British Admiralty enquiry commission on board *HMS Sister Anne*.

Above : defusing *Tellerminen* and shells placed on poles.

Obstacles known as "Czech Hedgehogs" on the beach of Ver-sur-Mer.

A Landing Craft Obstruction Clearance Units team on the beach at Bernières. The driver of the Jeep holds a shell. A Royal Marines commando is sat at the rear. One can see "Czech Hedgehogs" in the background.

Vehicles queue up on the beach of Ver-sur-Mer, waiting for the road to be free. On the left is an amphibious DUKW bogged down in the peat.

An amphibious DUKW vehicle completely bogged down in the layer of clay present beneath the pebbles on the La Rivière beach.

39. Hitler's spy plane photographs the beaches at high altitude

This was the very first wartime mission for a jet plane. On 2 August 1944, the Arado Ar 234 took off from Juvincourt in the Aisne in order to undertake a high altitude flight over the frontline, from Normandy to Brittany.

On 2 August 1944, the weather was fine over the *Luftwaffe* base at Juvincourt, in the Aisne. The same could be said over the Normandy front, notably over Arromanches and the allied airfields in the bridgehead. The order was given to undertake a first reconnaissance flight with the Arada Ar 234 jet, a plane that had carried out its maiden flight five months earlier on 10 March of the same year.

Oberleutnant Erich Sommer climbed into his aircraft via the front right hand side canopy. The plane had been lifted onto its take-off trolley. The technicians carried out their final checks. Previously towed out by a tractor onto the *Rollstrasse* (the taxiway to the runway) from its earth bank protected shelter, the Ar 234 was led onto to the concrete runway. Propeller powered escort fighters, Messerschmitt Bf 109 and Focke-Wulf 190 warmed up their engines. They were tasked with accompanying the Arado when it took off and upon its return, both of which were critical moments at which this revolutionary aircraft could be shot down by an enemy fighter.

In his cockpit, once he arrived at his take-off point at the end of the runway, Sommer, still assisted by the last technicians, started the jet engines with the help of an auxiliary Rieden AK 11 engine that was tasked with starting the jet engine vanes.

Men equipped with fire hoses were ready to intervene in the event of a problem. Sommer had little room to move in the jet aircraft. To his left, the two throttles had to be used with a delicate touch; these were used to control the engines that he allowed to rev up. He ran a final check of his flaps, rudder and elevator controls. A quick look outside showed him that everything was okay. Once his radio was plugged in, he followed the control tower's instructions.

Ready for take-off. Slowly, the plane began moving with a strange whistling sound. The inhabitants of Juvincourt, more used to the sound of propellers, watched from far as the plane headed towards the west. A brief shudder and the trolley came loose and fell away, slowed down by a parachute. To be safe, the three landing skids remained deployed in case of an aborted take-off. The skids were retracted and Sommer saw the German fighters which accompanied him.

Checking the numerous control instruments, the pilot gained altitude and finally reached a height of twelve thousand metres where he would be safe from Flak (*Flug-Abwehr-Kanonen*, anti-aircraft), and any fighters, except a few aircraft reserved for guarding Great Britain, such as the stratospheric Spitfires could reach.

At eight-hundred kilometres per hour, it did not take long to fly from the Aisne department to Normandy. Before reaching his objective, the pilot prepared his photographic equipment (Rb 50/30 cameras). Placed in front of him, a

An amazing document: The original flight plan for the Arado flown by Horst Götz, for its transfer from Germany to Juvincourt, on 2 August 1944, in view of its flight over the Western Front.

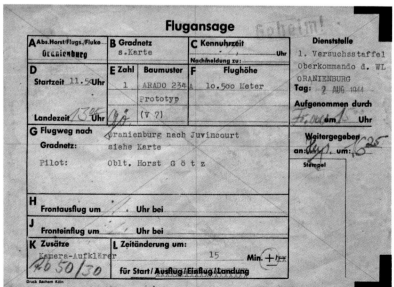

General characteristics Arado Ar 234

Powerplant: 2 x Jumo 004 B-0 Type: turbojet engines each with 8.83kN thrust	Average speed: 760 km/h approximately (Note that Erich Sommer reached a speed of 950
Wingspan: 14.20 m	km/h during a dive carried out on flight N°2 on 26 June 1944)
Length: 12.56 m	Service ceiling: 10,000 m
Height: 3.81 m	Range: 800 km approximately
Wing area: 26.4 m2	Armament: none
Weights: 4,750 kg (empty) 8,700 kg (maximum)	Photographic equipment: 2 x Rb50/30

Arado Ar 234 with its take-off trolley and skids. (Profile by Thierry Vallet.)

TVallet
© Thierry Vallet

Above: Arado Ar 234 taking off. Take off was carried out with a three-wheeled trolley which was jettisoned and then slowed down by a parachute.

To Philippe

Opposite: Erich Sommer in 1942. He sent this signed photo to Philippe Bauduin in the 2000s when he was living in Australia. Sommer and Götz remained together throughout the entire war.

Below: Horst Götz seen here in his Junkers Ju-86 R "T5+PM" with which he flew, accompanied by Erich Sommer, the first stratospheric combat flight in history, on 12 September 1942, against the specially modified Spitfire Mk IX flown by Prince Emmanuel Galitzine. These three aviators all flew in France in August 1944.

periscope allowed him to see the vapour trails. If there were too many, these would dangerously attract the attention of anti-aircraft guns.

Sommer looked at his map and began taking photos. Below was the war, or almost, as the Arromanches zone was no more than a supply base, but one that was essential to feeding the gigantic allied war machine. Meticulously, the German pilot made three passes, photographing airfields where the famous "Typhoon" tank-killer planes were based, troopships, boats and even the few fields that had remained unscathed by the June attack. It was now time to return to base. A very long turn was made to prevent fatiguing the plane's structure that was placed under great stress at such an altitude, then the flight towards the east and Juvincourt.

A high altitude photo taken by Erich Sommer whilst flying his Arado Ar 234, 2 August 1944. This is an amazing document as it was strictly forbidden for a pilot to take a camera on board.

The Arado Ar 234 flying over the landing beaches in August 1944. (Painting Barry Spicer.)

Everything had gone according to plan. Above Soissons, the Arado, starting to lose altitude, met up with the fighters sent to protect it.

Juvincourt was in sight. Somme lowered the long central landing skid, as well as the others, under the jet engines. He reduced speed and lowered the flaps. He had been gone for an hour and a half. Slowly, and no doubt in radio contact with the operator tasked with guiding him towards the grass runway, he gradually descended: two-hundred, one-hundred, fifty metres, then twenty, ten, he shut down the engines. Thanks to a *Luftwaffe* archive film, we can see that the landing was very hard,

the plane slid at speed. The pilot deployed his braking parachute, then the long slide across the grass came to an end. The three skids had held!

Men ran towards the immobilised plane. In his cockpit, pilot officer Sommer unclipped his oxygen mask, then took in a deep breath, all the time remaining in his seat. He saw his comrades smiling at him through the canopy. Assisted by one of the Arado technicians, he took off the straps that had held him down firmly throughout the flight.

Outside the plane, the sun dazzled him for an instant. Some people pushed forward to shake his hand. After all, was this not the world's first ever reconnaissance flight by a jet-powered plane? More than this, it was the first ever wartime flight by this type of aircraft!

This mission would be carried out several other times between 2 and 12 August 1944, either by Erich Sommer or Horst Götz, the other pilot tasked with missions flying the Ar 234. In the evening, when the German jet plane passed above them, the allied pilots spoke into their radios: *"It's bedtime Charley..."*. But Charley carried on undisturbed, safe and sound up there.

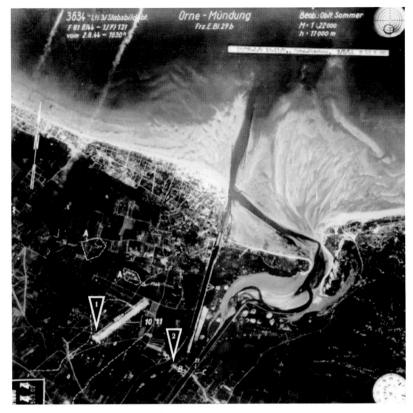

DT/TM-4/W 10-11/F., Orne-Mundung, Data Sheet

Auswerter:	Filmkennung:	Aufnahmedatum:	Beobachter:
Fw.Herold	F 81 L/44 1.(F)121	2.8.44-16.30	Oblt.Sommer
			F.A.G.123
Bildnr.144	Frz.E.Bl.29b		M = 1 : 22 000
3634 - Lfl.3			h = 11 000 m

O r n e - M ü n d u n g

10 11 = Landefläche Quistreham, Länge 1080 m
          Belegung nicht erkennbar
    A = Befestigungsanlagen
    B = Behelfsbrücken
          alt gegenüber Vergleichsbild 3548-Lfl.3vv.7.7.44
    C = Behelfsbrücke, neu gegenüber Vergleichsbild
   18 = 5 Hafen- und Küstenfahrzeuge
   25 = 1 Landungsfähre
    a = etwa 50 Lastensegler

                                              Stabsbildabteilung 3

Above : Ouistreham and the Orne estuary. On the left bank of the canal, one can see the airfield of Saint- Aubin-d'Arquenay (1) which was not used by RAF combat units, but for the re-despatching to England of gliders released over the right side of the Orne canal. These dismantled gliders crossed over either Pegasus Bridge, or over the boat bridge that can be seen south of the lock (2). Re-assembled at Saint-Aubin-d'Arquenay, they returned to the other side of the Channel, towed by DC3 aircraft. They would be used again during Operation Market Garden in Holland, mid-September.

Document for the interpretation of the Ouistreham and Orne estuary photo.

Pegasus Bridge. One can see the gliders used for the raid carried out by British paratroopers on the bridge and which were dismantled and re-despatched to England via Saint-Aubin-d'Arquenay.

Opposite: after Asnelles, which was only an emergency airfield, Sainte-Croix-sur-Mer was the first airbase built near the coast (1). With construction beginning on 8 June, its first aircraft, a Typhoon, landed on 10 June. On 13 June, two squadrons of RAF Free French pilots, the Alsace group and the *groupe Alsace* and *groupe Île-de-France*, landed at Sainte-Croix-sur-Mer in order to fly sorties over Normandy before returning to England. Only the Spitfire flown by Denys Boudard, remained in France overnight due to mechanical problems caused by the dust. The pilot spent the night in the village hall-school at Sainte-Croix-sur-Mer. On the morning of 15 June, Eisenhower's B-17 Flying Fortress landed on the one thousand two-hundred metre long runway.

```
        DT/TM-L/W 10-8/F., Ver-Sur-Mer, Data Sheet
Auswe                                      
Uffz. Münch    F 81 3/44      2.8.44        Oblt.Sommer
               1.(F)121      16.30  Uhr
Bildnr.: 134          Frz.%.Bl. 29         M  = 1 :22000
Lfl.3 - 3623                               h  = 11000 m

                Ver  -  sur  -  Mer
                ( 13 km nordost Bayeux)

1o 3 =  Flugplatz Ver-sur-Mer
        Belegung: a = 71 einmot. Flugzeuge
    1 =  Startbahn, etwa 1100 m
    2 =  Rollstraßen
    A =  Zeltlager mit etwa 3oo Rundzelten und
         3o Hauszelte
    B =  Materialstapel
    3 =  Panzergraben
    4 =  etwa 2oo Kraftfahrzeuge
    5 =  Splitterschutzgräben für Kraftfahrzeuge

                              Stabsbildabteilung  3
```

Above: the interpretive document for the Ver-sur-Mer photograph.

Wednesday 2 August 1944, 16.30 hrs. Flying his Arado 234 at an altitude of 11,000 metres, Erich Sommer photographs the "Mulberry B" artificial port (Arromanches-Asnelles). This photo, seemingly sent by wire photo to the German headquarters, reveals the presence of floating pontoons and more than three-hundred ships.

```
 Auswerter:     Filmkennung:    Aufnahmedatum:    Beobachter:
Pfefferkorn,Uffz.  F 81 R L/44    2.8.44 - 16.30 Uhr  Oblt.Sommer
                   1.(F)121
Bildnr.F 81 R /44 -127,129     Frz.2.Bl.29      M = 1:22 000
       F 81 L/44 -129                           h = 11 000 m
3617-Lfl.3          S c h i f f s a n s a m m l u n g

                 nördl. A s n e l l e s -sur-Mer

Kriegsschiffe:  4 =  1 Zerstörer
                6 = 30 Schnellboote
               6a =18 Artillerie-Schnellboote
                8 = 18 Geleitboote
                9 = 20 Minenfahrzeuge

Landungsschiffe:
               11 =  5 LST
              12a =  6 LCT 120 t
              12b =  6 LCT 350 t
              13a =  8 verm. LCM
               13 = 60 Kleinlandungsboote, Typ nicht
                       erkennbar.
               14 = 70 Hilfslandungsboote

Handelsschiffe:
               15 =  1 Truppentransporter,  etwa 10 000 BRT
               16 =  9 Frachter,     zus. "  32 000 BRT
              16a =25 Einheitsfrachter, "   " 175 000 BRT
               17 =  1 Tanker            "   "  10 000 BRT
                     Gesamttonnage etwa 247 000 BRT

Sonstige Belegung:
               18 = 30 Hafen-u.Küstenfahrzeuge
               23 =  1 verm. Begleitschiff, etwa 175 m lang
               24 =  5 Landungsstege
              24a =  Teile für Landungsstege
               25 = 72 zusammengesetzte Molenteile

                                         wenden!
```

The interpretive document for the Asnelles-Arromanches photograph.

Like all the other *Luftwaffe* photos, those taken by the Arados flown by Sommer and Götz over Normandy were archived at Berlin-Tempelhof. They were captured by the Soviet army in 1945 and stored in barges for future analysis in the USSR. Finding themselves in the US sector following the division of the capital into four parts, the barges in question were recovered by the Americans as part of Operation Dick Tracey and transferred to the United States.

Later, when the Soviet authorities asked for the famous photos, they were told that unfortunately, the barges had been set on fire and had sunk. Hidden away in the Washington National Archives, they were found there after the fall of the Berlin Wall. Out of the some five thousand photos taken during thirteen sorties over Normandy and Brittany throughout the summer of 1944, sadly only thirty remain at NARA in Washington. It is likely that the US Air Force has a few here and there...

Longues-sur-Mer. At the top left of the runway, numerous bomb and shell holes surround the batteries (1). To the right is the Manvieu cape and the port of Arromanches (2).

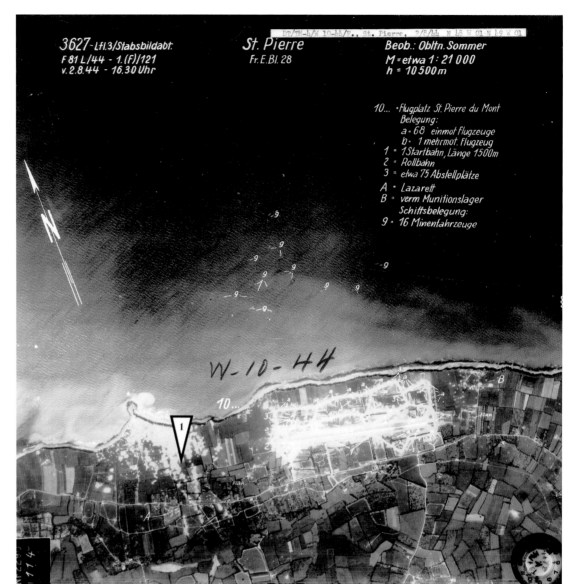

3627-Lfl.3/Stabsbildabt:
F 81 L/44 - 1. (F)/121
v. 2.8.44 - 16.30 Uhr

St. Pierre
Fr. E.Bl. 28

Beob.: Obltn. Sommer
M = etwa 1 : 21 000
h = 10 500 m

DT/TN-L/W 10-44/F., St. Pierre, 2/8/44 N 48 W 01 N 49 W 01

10... -Flugplatz St. Pierre du Mont
Belegung:
a - 68 einmot. Flugzeuge
b - 1 mehrmot. Flugzeug
1 = 1 Startbahn, Länge 1500 m
2 = Rollbahn
3 = etwa 75 Abstellplätze
A = Lazarett
B = verm. Munitionslager
Schiffsbelegung:
9 = 16 Minenfahrzeuge

Saint-Pierre-Du-Mont. To the west of this big US Air Force base, we have a striking view of the Pointe du Hoc, one of D-Day's most famous places, literally ploughed up by bombs and shells. The "V" seen to the south-east of Pointe du Hoc (1) represents the impacts caused by the shellfire of two warships.

An Arado Ar 234 captured by the Americans and seen here at the Wright Field airbase.

Opposite: a Jumo 004 turbine vane made with Chromadur Krupp.

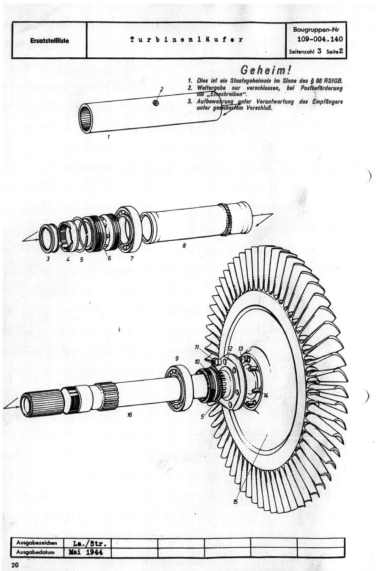

Above: vanes being mounted in a Jumo 004 jet engine turbine.

Above: a close-up of the turbine on its Junkers Jumo 004 turbojet axis that powered the Arado 234. This May 1944-dated German technical document is stamped *Geheim* (secret). The Jumo 004 was the first turbojet to go into large-scale production. As well as the Arado 234, it powered the Messerschmitt Me 262 fighter.

© Thierry Vallet

A front view of the Arado Ar 234. (Profile by Thierry Vallet.)

Contents

Photo taken from a "top secret" British report (see chapter 38).

Photo taken from a "top secret" British report (see chapter 38).

Bibliography

Le Secret du Jour J, Gilles Perrault, Fayard

Histoire du Débarquement, Carlo d'Este, Perrin

Histoire du Débarquement en Normandie, Olivier Wieviorka, Le Seuil

Histoire secrète des stratagèmes de la Seconde Guerre mondiale, Jean Deuve, Nouveau Monde

Seule face à l'Abwehr, Lily Sergueiew, Fayard

La Luftwaffe face au débarquement allié, Jean-Bernard Frappé, Heimdal

Les pilotes français du 6 juin 1944, François Robinard, Heimdal

Sur le sentier de la guerre, les Indiens d'Amérique dans la guerre 1939-1945, Stéphane Jacquet, Heimdal

Guerres et Découvertes, Philippe Bauduin, OREP

L'or rouge, Philippe Bauduin, Cheminements

Normandie 1944, Arado, l'avion espion, Philippe Bauduin, Heimdal

Commando Kieffer, les Français débarquent en Normandie, Jean-Charles Stasi, Heimdal

Bayeux 1944, Georges Bernage, Heimdal

Acknowledgements

Musée du Grand Bunker (Ouistreham), Musée de la résistance bretonne (Saint-Marcel), Jacques Clémentine, Patrick Collet, Dominique Forget (Archives de Guerre), Jean-Bernard Frappé, Stéphane Jacquet, Corinne et Gérard Liard, François Robinard, Famille Schloesing, Thierry Vallet.

Photo taken from a "top secret" British report (see chapter 38).

Printed in France in April 2017 by the Champagne printers at Langres (52) for Éditions Heimdal, Georges Bernage, publisher.